S   itionist
a   um of
two hung_   ... personal experience
how hard it can be to juggle work and fami___   still
provide healthy m_ _ar__ __   _other
to really mak_   _n and
to ensure that __   __ _ver wasted. In this book,
she shows _ w careful planning can transform the
way yo_ _ok and actually free you up to enjoy more
relaxing _me with your family.

THE BUSY MUM'S PLAN-AHEAD COOKBOOK

Sarah Flower

ROBINSON

ROBINSON

First published in Great Britain in 2014 by Robinson

A CIP catalogue record for this book
is available from the British Library.

ISBN: 978-1-84528-537-1 (paperback)
ISBN: 978-1-84528-560-9 (ebook)

Typeset in Baskerville by PJM Design
Printed and bound in Great Britain by CPI Mackays

Robinson
is an imprint of
Constable & Robinson Ltd
100 Victoria Embankment
London EC4Y 0DY

An Hachette UK Company
www.hachette.co.uk

www.constablerobinson.com

Contents

HOW TO USE THIS BOOK

Juggling a busy working life with children can be a massive challenge, add to this the need for healthy food, and you start to frazzle under the pressure. This book draws upon the experiences I have had being a parent and also the experiences of my mum – an accomplished cook in her own right.

I was brought up in the 1970s in a working-class family. Dad worked long hours and Mum juggled part-time work with being a parent. Processed food was expensive and seen to be more of a luxury than necessity so we always had home-cooked, economical meals. Mum and I would spend Sundays cooking the roast alongside the cakes and savouries for the following week. We had a large chest freezer that was used constantly. We also had a vegetable garden and an allotment, allowing us to eat fresh, seasonal vegetables. It was hard work but if we draw upon this knowledge we can find ways to dramatically lessen our time in the kitchen while still providing our families with home-cooked, healthy meals, saving us time and money.

One of the main concepts of this recipe book is to use your time wisely. Using a slow cooker and your freezer can save you time and money. Learn how to double up your recipes to create your own ready meals or convert half of your dish into something different for another night – it really takes very little time to double up and planning ahead saves you lots of time.

I would strongly advise that you read through the opening chapters of this book, as it will make much more sense to you in the long term. You do need to be organised to follow this principle but once you have started, you will soon find that it becomes second nature and suddenly you have lots more free time. On pages 245–63 you will find a quick reference to recipes and meal guides. Here you can search for slow cooker recipes, oven-cook or hob recipes, or look for recipes for packed lunches and those that can be frozen.

Start by getting to know the book and listing your family's favourite recipes. If these can be frozen, then make a note to double up the ingredients to make two or more dishes at the same time. You will find that this actually takes very little extra time, but when you are busy and you pull a homemade meal from the freezer you will feel extremely pleased with yourself! Always make sure that you label and date anything before popping it into the freezer. I would also advise you to search through your freezer at least once a month, making sure you bring the items that need using up first to the top.

Slow cookers are fantastic and really can save you lots of time. Remember, you can fill a slow cooker the night before or in the morning before you go to work. There are some slow cooker tips in this book to help get you started.

Menu plans can seem a bit of a faff to stick to but most of us repeat the same meals week after week so why not design your own? You can write your own supermarket shopping list to suit, as this will help you keep costs down. I have included a four-week menu planner and some tips at the back of this book (pages 245–63) to help get you started and to give you an idea of how they work.

One of the other golden rules in the book is to fill your oven! My mum was always fanatical about this – if you turn the oven on, it must be full to make the most of the energy you are using. This can be a great time to get ahead or to create your own treats and savouries for packed lunches or snacks. At the end of the book you'll find a list of recipes to cook in the oven (pages 257–60) so you can use these to help fill your oven when you have a baking session.

All the lists at the end of the book provide an easy reference to help you plan ahead. For example, if you particularly want to stock up your freezer, turn to the double up and freeze recipes (pages 260–62). Or if you just want to use your hob and not turn the oven on at all, turn to the list of hob and grill recipes (pages 259–60). Likewise, the list of slow cooker recipes (page 256) will make it easy for you to choose recipes that will cook themselves while you are at work.

I hope you enjoy the book and that it makes a big difference to you and your family.

Sarah Flower

STOCKING YOUR KITCHEN

As much as we would like to think otherwise, most of us have little idea what is lurking in our store cupboards, fridge and freezers. A friend of mine discovered a frozen chicken in her freezer that was eight years old! How can we possibly budget for food when we don't know what we have? This chapter will help to make sure that you always have food in the house to rustle up an impromptu meal, as well as minimising your waste, reducing your weekly food bill and maximising the results of your cooking efforts.

Store Cupboard Essentials

When I started looking at my household food budgets, I decided to make a checklist of the key foods in my kitchen (not store cupboard essentials or snacks). I then made a list of all the meals I could make using these ingredients. Altogether, I estimated I would have about five main meals. In fact, I managed to make eighteen substantial meals and nine puddings. I thought it would be fun to write these meals down and tick them off when I had made them. I then created a shopping list by adding the key ingredients I needed to replace. It was a revelation! I didn't have to think about what to cook; I simply went to my list and chose something I fancied. Over a period of two weeks I cut my shopping bill by over a third, without buying less or cheaper food.

Stocking a Good Store Cupboard

This is a list of foods that I will always have in my kitchen. Everyone's list will vary to some extent, but with a good store cupboard and a few key ingredients, you'll always be able to rustle up a great meal.

I always make sure that these items are replaced when I use or finish something. Just looking at the lists below I could, in an emergency, make several meals without having to go shopping.

Fruit and Vegetables

- Onions
- Garlic – including ready-crushed as a standby
- Potatoes – keep better if stored in potato sacks
- Peppers – red, yellow and green
- Carrots
- Ginger – If you have any fresh that needs using up, slice thinly and place in a jar, topped up with white wine vinegar.

Herbs and Spices

- Paprika
- Garam masala
- Sweet curry
- Curry paste
- Chilli powder or freeze-dried chilli
- Ground cinnamon
- Ground coriander
- Ground ginger
- Nutmeg
- Mixed spice
- Turmeric
- Mixed herbs
- Dried bay leaves

Store Cupboard Basics

- Baked beans
- Rice – long grain and pudding rice
- Pasta
- Flour – plain and self-raising
- Sugar
- Tomato purée
- Tinned tomatoes
- Red lentils
- Soup mix
- Oats
- Olive oil – the best quality you can afford
- Stock cubes
- Dried fruit

- Chocolate, cocoa and chocolate chips
- Balsamic vinegar, lemon juice and soy sauce
- White and red wine
- White and red wine vinegar
- Salt
- Pepper (black or white)

Optional Extras

- Ready-made pasta or curry sauce – great if you want a quick and easy meal. Stock up when jars are on offer.
- Bread flour and dried yeast
- Tinned tuna
- Passata (sieved tomatoes)

Fridge Store

- Cheese
- Eggs
- Milk
- Butter or margarine

- Natural yoghurt
- Crème fraîche (optional)
- Quark

Storage Tip

According to experts, cheese should be stored wrapped in waxed paper and not in plastic bags or packaging.

Freezer Store

- Peas and other vegetables
- Puff pastry
- Mince
- Bread and bread rolls
- Chicken
- Sausages
- Frozen herbs

Alternative to cheese

Nutritional yeast flakes are a useful store cupboard essential, whether or not you are a vegan. If you are looking to cut down on your intake of cheese, nutritional yeast flakes give a 'cheesy' flavour to sauces and savoury dishes such as quiches. The flakes are packed with B vitamins. Found in health food stores, they are relatively inexpensive to buy.

Storing Fresh Fruit and Vegetables

Now you have your store cupboard sorted, you need to work out how to get the best out of your food. Think about where you are storing your fresh fruit and vegetables. Traditionally, homes would have a cool pantry or larder, which was great for keeping things fresh. Apples would be stored to last the whole winter, yet we struggle to get them to last a week. Supermarkets may have had the produce for weeks before it reaches you, thereby losing valuable nutrients and shortening its useful life, so it is always best to buy fresh from your local farmers' market, pannier market or green grocer. as their supply chain will be shorter.

Bananas

If you want them to last, buy green. Never store bananas in the fridge, but do try to keep them in a cool place, and away from touching other fruit as they emit a gas that speeds up the ripening process. You can buy special bags to store bananas. One online store, Lakeland (www.lakeland.co.uk), offers a great banana storage bag: when kept in the fridge, it provides bananas with the exact amount of insulation and air needed to stop the flesh over-ripening, while keeping the skin warm enough to prevent it blackening. Amazingly, the fruit will stay just as it should for around a fortnight – twice its normal lifespan. You can also freeze bananas. I freeze bananas that are starting to brown (knowing my boys won't touch them like this). Freeze them in the skin then peel them before use in smoothies, cakes or baked banana puddings.

Mushrooms

Although most supermarkets sell mushrooms in those horrible plastic containers, they should be placed in paper bags and stored in the fridge. Kept in plastic, the mushrooms will produce moisture and very quickly start to rot. As with bananas, you can buy bags for mushrooms which do work well, and may be worth the investment if you regularly buy and store mushrooms.

Root vegetables

Keep these in a dry, cool, dark place. If you do not have an area suitable, store them in your fridge, but not in the plastic packaging. Placing an old tea towel on the bottom shelf of the fridge shelf will help to avoid moisture spoiling the food. Potatoes keep best in dark, cool places. Never leave them in plastic, though paper bags are fine.

Salad

Bagged salad leaves are very expensive as well as damaging to the environment when you consider the packaging and processing involved, so try to avoid them or – if you do buy them – take care not to let them go to waste. Out of season, buy lettuce whole (Iceberg seems to be the longest-lasting). Store all salad items in your fridge, out of plastic and away from moisture. Again, you can use the tea-towel trick described above to combat moisture. Cucumbers and tomatoes should be firm when you buy them. If you like your tomatoes with lots of flavour, keep them at room temperature, in a bowl: they will only last three to four days but will be tastier than tomatoes stored in the fridge.

Fruit

As with all fruit and vegetables, store in a cool, dry place. This sounds obvious, but I have walked into houses with fruit bowls next to radiators, or in front of windows. If you are worried about fruit spoiling or not lasting for long, store it in the fridge.

Strawberries

These never taste the same out of season, so save yourself, and enjoy them when they are at their summer best. Never buy punnets that already contain mouldy fruit, as this will speed up the ripening process of the rest of the batch. Store in the fridge until you are ready to eat them, but remember to take them out at least an hour before serving, as this improves the flavour.

Making the Most of Your Freezer

The freezer is one of your main assets when planning your time in the kitchen. Years ago people opted for large chest freezers in a bid to save as much time and money as possible, but over the last twenty-five years, we have seen a decline in the need for these large freezers as more and more families have switched to using fresh produce, processed food and takeaways. We have, however, also seen a rise in waste. Currently almost a third of our weekly food ends up in the dustbin. Using a bit of savvy and a more frugal head, you can make the most of your freezer, fridge and store cupboard, avoid waste and save money.

Freezers make sense of the supermarket Buy One/Get One Free (BOGOF) deals – as long as you remember to include bulk purchases in your future weekly menu plans. You can fill your freezer with bargains, food grown on your allotment, and with homemade ready meals. Remember, freezers work more efficiently when used at capacity, so keep them well-stocked, but make a note of what is going in them. If you are placing home-produced items, label them with contents and date. The bigger the freezer, the easier it is to lose track of the contents and end up wasting your money and effort. I would recommend having a clear out of your freezer every month and bring what needs to be used to the top.

Storage Tip

Always label and date everything that goes into the freezer, this way you will know at a glance what you have and how long it has been lurking in the bottom of your freezer.

Why freeze food?

The concept is not new – we are just adopting the principle used by our grandparents and their parents before them. If you are preparing one meal, double up the recipe and you have two meals with minimal effort. Freeze this extra meal as a whole or in individual portions and soon you are on your way to saving yourself a whole load of time and energy! Imagine coming home from work and all you have to do is dig into your freezer to pull out a homemade lasagne. Friends pop by unannounced? Don't even break a sweat, pop some savoury pastries into the oven straight from the freezer. It is a simple concept that saves you so much time, but you do need to have a big enough freezer and you must plan ahead.

Get prepared

Start saving your old containers. I wash out and use margarine tubs, small milk cartons, yoghurt pots and ice-cube trays (preferably silicon as they 'pop' out easier). I also have sets of Tupperware and plastic containers picked up from boot sales and when discounted in stores. Remember, if you are going to microwave the contents at a later date, the containers need to be both microwave and freezer-safe. I buy foil containers with lids from our local pound shop in individual and larger portion sizes, and these can be used in the oven for reheating the food – you can also write on the lids with a permanent marker.

Always remember to label and date items you are placing in the fridge or freezer, and ideally, plan when you are going to use them. You really don't want to have bits and pieces of food in your freezer longer than a few months.

Recipes

All the recipes in this book include information about the number of people they serve and details about freezing. Some recipes can be frozen at the end of the recipe, some frozen in the uncooked state, or some, like iced cakes, are frozen at an earlier stage and completed once they have thawed.

Be freezer-friendly

Meat, fish and ready meals are often the most expensive things we buy, so move them straight into the freezer for another occasion if you don't think you'll have time to eat them or cook them before they go off in the fridge. Buying large quantities of meat can often be economical. Just divide the big packs into meal-sized portions, label them and freeze.

Wrapping food well before storing in the freezer will prevent freezer burn and help it to last as long as possible. Most foods can be frozen, including milk, cream, cheese, bread, cakes and tomatoes. A magnetic list on the freezer is a great way of keeping tabs on what you have in there, then once something comes out of the freezer, cross it off the list.

Keeping Safe

Many shop-bought meals can be frozen, but make sure that you freeze these by the 'use by' date at the very latest, and do not keep the item for longer than recommended on the label. When heating up, the food should be heated thoroughly until it reaches a minimum temperature of 70°C for at least two minutes, so that it is steaming hot. Contrary to popular belief, freezing does not kill all bacteria; it just slows down their growth. So minimise the risk of food poisoning by following these tips.

Before freezing:
- Make sure that all hot foods have been cooled quickly and thoroughly.
- Wrap each food item properly using a clean freezer bag or sealable container.
- Divide the food into appropriately sized portions.
- Label and date each item.

When defrosting:
- Speed up the process by using the 'defrost' facility on your microwave.
- Avoid the risk of cross-contamination by defrosting any meat, poultry or fish within its own sealed container or bowl at the bottom of the fridge, so no fluids drip onto other foods.
- Once the food has defrosted, use it immediately.

Do not:
- Freeze food more than once.Cook raw poultry or large joints of meat straight from frozen.

Generally, if you are following your menu planner, you can simply take your frozen meals/ingredients out from the freezer the night before, and leave these to defrost in the bottom of the fridge overnight. But make sure they are thoroughly defrosted before cooking, unless the recipe says that you can cook from frozen.

─── **Storage Tip** ───

Always take care to defrost poultry, fish and meat (and all dishes containing these) thoroughly before cooking.

Understanding food dates

Foods can be eaten or frozen right up until the end of the 'use by' date. Check the label on perishable items to see if they can be frozen. Many foods with a 'best before' date should be safe to eat after this date, just use your own judgement.

Use-by This is the key date in terms of safety. Never eat products after this date and observe all storage instructions strictly. Check if the food can be frozen if you need to eat it at a later date. 'Use by' dates are usually found on chilled products, such as cooked meats, soft cheeses and dairy-based desserts.

Best before 'Best before' dates are usually found on longer shelf-life foods, such as frozen, tinned or dried goods, and refer to quality rather than safety. So, with these items, it's best to use your judgement. It may be safe to eat food after the 'best before' date, but food may no longer be at its best.

Display until/Sell by Date marks such as 'display until' or 'sell by' often appear near or next to the 'best before' or 'use by' date. They are used by some shops to help with stock control and are instructions for shop staff, not shoppers.

Foods to freeze

Here are some ideas of everyday items to freeze that will help to make your kitchen run smoothly. It is really frustrating to throw away half-empty jars, tubes, tins or loaves of bread. Well, now you don't have to. In my freezer I have an area for homemade ready meals and another for frozen 'ingredients' like these.

Herbs

If you love cooking, you probably use a lot of fresh herbs. If you are able to grow your own you can chop and freeze any surplus herbs for later in the year. Some herbs go limp when frozen, but will still maintain their flavour. Herbs that freeze well are oregano, sage, dill, rosemary, mint, lemon grass, tarragon and thyme. I also freeze fresh chillies, garlic and ginger. You can buy freshly frozen herbs too. Some supermarkets sell 75g resealable bags of herbs and seasonings, which can last you months and offer a superior taste over dried varieties. Simply use what you want and pop the rest back into the freezer. They're perfect for adding to soups and casseroles.

Bread

Stale or leftover bread can be turned into breadcrumbs and then frozen. Spread it out on a tray and freeze like this to avoid clumping, then place in a container or freezer bag for storage. French sticks or speciality breads and bread rolls can go stale very quickly. Freeze them, then revitalise with a few splashes of water and bake in the oven for two to three minutes. Bread will usually keep in the freezer for up to three months.

Cheese

Here is an ideal tip for leftover cheeses, especially those we don't buy very often, such as blue cheese. You can grate them and freeze them spread out on a tray to avoid clumping, as page 12, before placing in a container or freezer bag. This is also ideal for Parmesan, as it lasts really well and avoids the smelly fridge scenario. Grated cheese can be frozen for up to four months and can be used straight from the freezer.

Pesto, pastes and purées

If, like me, you love spicy pastes and herb purées or pesto, place any leftovers in silicon ice-cube trays. These make it easy to pop out portion-sized dollops and freezing your leftovers avoids you finding mouldy jars in the back of your fridge, which then need to be thrown away. You can also freeze herb butters in portions like this.

Ripe avocados

Scoop out the flesh of ripe avocados and mix with a touch of lemon or lime juice before freezing. Once defrosted, use to make tasty dips.

Nuts and seeds

Nuts and even seeds can be frozen, but I tend to buy only what I need and store these in airtight jars.

Sweet potato

I sometimes have sweet potato in my vegetable tray that needs using up but don't have the desire or ingredients to immediately make use of it. To avoid waste, I chop them into usable chunks, coat with lemon juice to prevent discolouration, then place in a freezer bag to freeze. These chunks are ideal for adding to casseroles or soups when I don't have any fresh to hand.

Lemons

Sometimes recipes call for the zest and juice of half a lemon. You can squeeze the lemon juice from the remaining half and freeze it in ice-cube trays until needed, or why not cut the remaining lemon into slices or wedges and freeze for use in drinks – ice and a slice, all in one!

Pastry

Bought pastry does not have to be the only pastry in your freezer. Why not double up your batch of homemade pastry and freeze the leftovers for another day? Alternatively, think of some extra ways to use up the pastry – you could make mini tarts or pies and place them in the freezer ready as delicious nibbles for an impromptu drinks party, or to fill your packed lunch. Another great tip is to line some tinfoil pie cases and freeze them as empty pastry cases – these can then be filled with a quick quiche mixture or even a sweet dish. Raw pastry will freeze for up to six months.

Mashed potato

Overestimated your mashed potato? If you don't fancy making it into another recipe, you can freeze it in single portion sizes, ideal to reheat when you're in a hurry or to use as a topping for a pie.

Salsa

Leftover salsa? Freeze it in ice-cube trays, as page 13, then add a cube or two to spice up tomato pasta dishes.

Peppers

Deseed, chop, place in a freezer bag and freeze until needed.

Swede

Sometimes a swede can be too large for your immediate needs. Slice the unwanted swede into chunks, bag it, then place in the freezer until needed.

Bananas

Brown bananas are a prime candidate for waste, but you can freeze them for use in smoothies, or in baking. I simply pop them whole in the freezer, or peel and slice into a container and use as and when needed.

Curry, casseroles or pasta sauces

Leftover curry, casserole or pasta sauces can be frozen ready to be transformed into a new dish later on. Cool them quickly, then freeze straight away.

Ripe tomatoes

Chop ripe tomatoes and store in a container ready to use in tomato or pasta sauces. However, I prefer to slow bake them in the oven with garlic and herbs, then place in jars with some olive oil.

Berries

I absolutely love berries. My freezer is always well stocked with a variety of them ready for smoothies or delicious deserts. To freeze your own berries, place on a baking tray so they are not touching each other and freeze. Once frozen, you can then scoop them up and transfer to a freezer bag or other container for storage.

Vegetables

You can freeze most vegetables. The ideal way to freeze is to blanch the veg in boiling water for one to two minutes, then place in iced water to cool. Drain and pat dry before placing in freezer bags. Remember, you can use the cooking water as a base for homemade stock! Alternatively, why not make a delicious soup or casserole with your leftover vegetables, and then freeze it as a nutritious, homemade ready meal?

Pulses

In their dried form pulses will keep for months, but because rinsing, soaking and cooking them can be a bit of a faff, why not bulk cook and then freeze, ready to add to your favourite recipe?

Wine

If you have any wine left in the bottom of a bottle, freeze into small portions using ice-cube trays, ready to add to casseroles or pasta sauces.

Onion

Chopped onion can be frozen in a freezer bag and added to dishes when needed. This is also a great way to use up onions that are starting to turn.

Coconut milk

I love curries but find a whole can of coconut milk is not only fattening but also too rich to add to one dish. Instead I freeze in large ice-cube trays and just pop out a couple of cubes as and when needed.

Tortilla wraps

My eldest son is the only one who loves wraps, so one bag of ten inevitably ends up with wraps wasted. I now freeze the wraps and he defrosts them for thirty seconds under the grill before filling with whatever he chooses.

Lollipop, lollipop

Kids (and adults) love lollipops and ice-creams. I have some silicon ice-cream moulds which are easy to fill and form the perfect twirled ice-lollies. Fill these with leftover juices, smoothies or even custard!

Buttermilk

This can be frozen but it will separate so remember to whisk well once it has defrosted.

Bake one, bake one free

As I've already mentioned, my mum would never use the oven unless you could fill it up. If you are baking or being creative in the kitchen, why not double up and make more? You can then freeze one item, saving you time, energy and money. This is great for everyone, whether you are a single person or a family of four, as long as you have freezer space.

When baking with pastry, I always double up the recipes and place one uncooked pie or batch of pastry tarts in the freezer. Christmas is a great time to get ahead with a whole host of savoury and sweet pastry delights, making the most of your puff, filo and standard pastry.

Cakes and biscuits do freeze well. To avoid damaging the decoration if you are freezing a decorated cake or gâteau, freeze unwrapped until frozen before placing in a freezer bag or container.

Don't just freeze ingredients. You can also freeze whole meals, so learn to double up recipes. Meat, fish, poultry and vegetarian meals can all be frozen, though be aware of the correct reheating and defrosting procedures with meat, poultry and fish.

When parboiling potatoes ready to roast, why not double up and place one batch in the freezer for another day? Simply defrost gently, coat with your oil/paprika mix and place in a preheated oven. Some people coat the potatoes in the oil or herb mixture before freezing, so that they can be tipped straight into the roasting tray to go in the oven.

How to Use Your Leftovers

You would have to have had your head buried firmly in the sand if you have not heard about the amount of food we all waste every year. In some households it is commonplace to throw away almost one third of every week's grocery shop. If the average family spends £150 a week, that is £50 in the dustbin, which equates to a whopping £2,600 a year! Most of the food we throw away is from the fridge. Often this is not because there is anything wrong with it, but simply because we don't know how to use it up. Planning meals, and getting to know how to store food to make the most of it, could literally save you a small fortune each year.

The main wasted foods identified are fruit, cheese, vegetables and meat, all of which can be frozen or used if you plan ahead. But the food in our fridge is only a fraction of the waste in a household. How many of us have a roast chicken, but after carving simply throw the carcass away? The carcass will often have enough meat left on the bone and underneath to fill a pie or make a quick curry.

Throughout this book you will find ideas within the recipes to utilise your leftovers. On pages 7–17 there is also a section on how to use your freezer. Here you will find a list of common foods and ingredients you can freeze to save you time and money.

If you plan ahead with menu plans you should have very little waste. Think about your meals – for example, if you are making mashed potato for one meal, double up and use it for the next night as a topping for shepherd's pie. Making pastry? Double up and store in the fridge or freeze ready for your next baking session, or fill some pastry cases and freeze them ready to add a filling another time.

To stop fresh vegetables from going brown in the freezer, clean them, then pop them into a saucepan of boiling water for thirty seconds. Then, using a slotted spoon, scoop them out into a bowl of heavily iced water. Once chilled, drain the vegetables and dry them off using kitchen paper or a clean cloth. Now they are ready to freeze.

When cooking vegetables from frozen, use the microwave or a large pan of boiling water. Do not steam, as steaming makes frozen vegetables go soggy.

Here is a handy reference guide to leftover foods and how you can use them up.

LEFTOVER FOOD	IDEAS TO AVOID WASTE
Mashed potato	Use as a topping for meals such as shepherd's pie, make into cheese and onion pasties, potato croquettes, fish cakes, bubble and squeak.
Pastry	Transform into another dish, fill pastry cases ready to use (these can be frozen), freeze pastry in a freezer bag or keep refrigerated for three days.
Meat or chicken from a roast	Turn into curry, stir-fry, pies, casseroles, soups or pasties. There really are endless ways to use up meat and poultry so never throw this away.
Vegetables	When vegetables need using up you can make delicious soups, casseroles or freeze them. I freeze all vegetables – chopped onions, peppers, diced root veg – then just pull out handfuls whenever I need them to add to a recipe.
Cooked vegetables	Turn these into a quick soup or make a more traditional bubble and squeak. Leftover cooked potatoes can be transformed into a multitude of meals; my favourite use for leftover boiled or new potatoes is homity pie.
Herbs	If you have fresh herbs that need using up, mix them with some olive oil and place in ice-cube trays to freeze. These are also great to use as a herby oil for sautéeing. Alternatively, mix the fresh herbs with butter. You can pop this into ice-cube trays as above or form the butter into a sausage, cut into discs and freeze – these can be added to baked fish or again when you are sautéeing.

LEFTOVER FOOD	IDEAS TO AVOID WASTE
Fruit	Don't waste fruit – freeze bananas, kiwis, berries, mangos and melon, then use them in smoothies straight from the freezer. Frozen banana can also be used to make banana cake. I have placed frozen banana slices in an ovenproof dish, covered it with chocolate custard and then topped it with crumbled chocolate cake for a really decadent pudding! Apples, pears, plums and rhubarb can all be stewed, then frozen or made into delicious puddings, especially crumbles.
Custard	Whether you make your own or buy readymade, sometimes you have half a jug of custard left. Add some fruit and turn into ice lollies for the children.
Eggs	Some recipes ask only for egg yolk to be used. When this happens I pop the egg white into freezer bags and label how many egg whites it contains. I then use this to make meringues.
Tomatoes	Never throw these away! I'm a big fan of roasting tomatoes in garlic and herbs. I then use this as a base for a pasta sauce, topping for pizza or add to a casserole or any dish that uses tomatoes. You can place the roasted tomatoes in a sterilised jar and keep in the fridge for up to one week.
Bread	Again, don't throw this away. Whizz in your processor to make breadcrumbs. You can also freeze slices of bread ready to make bread and butter pudding or even summer pudding. This also works well with fruit bread or buns.

LEFTOVER FOOD	IDEAS TO AVOID WASTE
Cake	Do not throw away stale sponge cake. Use to make a trifle (or freeze down to use later) or cover with fruit and custard to make a quick, cheap pudding. You can also use ginger cake for this, which tastes great with mandarin oranges.
Biscuits	If plain biscuits have gone soft, you can revive them by placing in a hot oven for a few minutes and cooling on a rack. You can also use up the broken bits by making a base for a cheesecake. To prevent biscuits going soft in a tin, place a cube of sugar in with them. The sugar absorbs moisture, thus making your biscuits last longer.
Bacon	If you have a couple of rashers left after a cooked breakfast, do not just put them to the back of the fridge. Make a quiche with a pastry case you have stored in your freezer. You could also use it up in an omelette or frittata or add chopped bits to chicken casserole or soup.
Salad bags	We are all guilty of using only half a bag of salad leaves from time to time. If you cannot use the leftovers the next day, maybe for a packed lunch, put it into soups or casseroles.
Crisps	A squashed packet of crisps or left-over tortilla crisps? Use them for a crispy topping on a savoury dish or even crushed to make a crispy coating for your homemade fish fingers.

LEFTOVER FOOD	IDEAS TO AVOID WASTE
Cereal	Left-over cereal in the bottom of the pack but not enough to fill a bowl? My children love to mix and match so we have a container where the cereal gets mixed up. You can also use leftover cereal in cakes, crumbles (as a topping), or toppings for savoury dishes (cornflakes work brilliantly for this).
Lemonade	Lemonade gone flat? Freeze it in ice-lolly moulds. Lemonade is also great to use as a plant food for fresh-cut flowers or houseplants.
Cola	Flat cola? Again, you can pour it into ice-lolly moulds and freeze.
Wine	Never throw wine away – save it for cooking as it adds an amazing flavour. You can also freeze wine: I use silicon ice-cube moulds as I can then pop a cube or three into a dish (one cube is roughly one tablespoon).
Milk	Milk that needs using up can be frozen, or why not cook something with it? Rice pudding, custards, white sauce or cheese sauce – anything you use regularly can be made and frozen.

LIGHT MEALS AND SNACKS

This chapter contains recipes for light meals and snacks, as well as a range that can be used for picnics and packed lunches. Refer to the Quick Reference Guide (pages 256–63) to find the recipe you need.

Always remember the golden rule – if you are turning on your oven, fill it up! So, if you are making a roast or oven dish for a main meal, refer back to this chapter for some quick and easy savouries that you can cook for the week ahead. Some can be prepared in advance, some can be frozen, so double up the recipe and freeze one to always be one step ahead on a busy midweek evening.

All the recipes here can be served with crusty bread to make a warm, filling meal.

Red Tomato, Pepper and Sweet Potato Soup

This velvety soup is smooth and satisfying, with a rich, deep flavour coming from the vine tomatoes. Add a splash of chilli oil to give it a kick.

PLAN AHEAD
Slow cooker recipe
Double up
and freeze

Serves 4

2 red onions, cut into thick wedges

2 red peppers, deseeded and cut into thick wedges

1 sweet potato, thickly sliced

3 garlic cloves, left whole

250–300g vine tomatoes, skinned and chopped

½ tsp dried thyme

400ml low-salt vegetable stock or water

Seasoning to taste

Chilli oil to serve

1   Cut the vegetables into equal-size chunks so that they will cook evenly.

2   If your slow cooker needs to be preheated, turn it on 15 minutes before using. Refer to your manufacturer's instructions for more information on your specific model temperatures.

3   Put all the ingredients into the slow cooker. Make sure the stock is hot when adding, as this will help to get the soup up to temperature quickly.

4   Cook on low for 6 hours or if you want a faster meal, turn to high for 4 hours.

5   Liquidise gently using an electric stick blender until the soup is smooth. Allow to cool before freezing.

6   Serve with a drizzle of chilli oil.

Top Tip

Use tinned tomatoes instead of fresh, if preferred. I recommend good-quality tinned tomatoes such as Italian cherry tomatoes. Add 2 teaspoons of sun-dried tomato paste for rich flavour.

Healthy Tip

This soup is rich in lycopene and antioxidants. Lycopene is more easily absorbed by the body when the tomatoes are cooked.

Carrot and Courgette Soup

Ginger adds a lovely zing to this soup. If I feel like I need more of a hit, I add one or two fresh chillies, deseeded and finely chopped.

PLAN AHEAD
Hob recipe
Double up
and freeze

Serves 4–6

Spray of olive oil

1 red onion, chopped

2–3 carrots, diced

1 sweet potato, diced

1–2 tsp grated fresh ginger

600ml low-salt-vegetable stock

1 tsp dried or fresh thyme

2–3 courgettes, diced

1   Cook the onion in olive oil in a saucepan until soft and translucent.

2   Add the carrots and sweet potato and cook for a couple of minutes to soften. Add the fresh ginger and cook for another minute.

3   Add all the remaining ingredients, place on low heat and cook slowly for 30–40 minutes.

4   You can leave the soup as is, or cool slightly and use an electric stick blender to purée until smooth. Allow to cool before freezing. Reheat when you are ready to serve.

Chunky Winter Vegetable and Lentil Soup

This is a fabulous soup for using up any vegetables you may have that are past their best. Remember to cut them into equal sizes so that they cook evenly.

PLAN AHEAD
Slow cooker recipe
Double up
and freeze

Serves 4

1 red onion, finely chopped

1 large carrot, diced

2 sweet potatoes, diced

1 leek, finely chopped

1 parsnip, diced

1 potato, diced

2 sticks of celery, diced

1 litre of low-salt or homemade vegetable or chicken stock

2 garlic cloves, crushed

1 bay leaf

75g red lentils

½ tsp dried parsley

1   If your slow cooker needs to be preheated, turn it on 15 minutes before using. Refer to your manufacturer's instructions for more information on your specific model temperatures.

2   Put all the ingredients in the slow cooker. Make sure the stock is hot as this will help to get the soup up to temperature quickly.

3   Cook on low for 8–10 hours or, if you want a faster meal, turn to high for 5–6 hours.

4   Leave the soup chunky or, if you prefer, purée to a smooth texture. I like to remove two-thirds of the soup, purée the remaining third and then mix the two back together. This creates a creamy base for the chunky soup. Allow to cool thoroughly before freezing.

Extra Recipes

Double up this recipe, remove half before you blend the soup and top with finely sliced potatoes and a little grated cheese before freezing to make Chunky Winter Vegetable and Lentil Hotpot. To cook, defrost before popping in the oven at 190°C (gas mark 5) for 25 minutes until piping hot.

Healthy Tip

This dish delivers at least two portions of your five-a-day. It is packed with alliums (red onions, garlic, leeks)which can help to protect your joints from deterioration. The lentils provide protein and are bursting with magnesium, biotin, zinc and iron.

Chicken, Cumin and Harissa Soup

A lovely warming soup but chop everything evenly, as it's best left chunky.

PLAN AHEAD
Slow cooker recipe
Double up
and freeze

Serves 4–6

1 red onion, finely chopped

2–3 garlic cloves, finely chopped

1 red pepper, deseeded and finely chopped

1 tsp ground cumin

1 tsp paprika

2–3 tsp Harissa paste

400g tin of chickpeas, drained

400g tin of chopped tomatoes

400g chicken fillets, diced (thigh meat gives the best flavour)

500ml chicken stock

Large handful of freshly chopped coriander

Natural yoghurt or crème fraîche to serve

1   If your slow cooker needs preheating, turn it on 15 minutes before use. Refer to the manufacturer's instructions for more information on your specific model.

2   Add all the ingredients apart from the fresh coriander. Make sure the chicken stock is hot when adding as this will help the soup to reach the right temperature quickly.

3   Turn your slow cooker to auto and cook for 6–8 hours. If you don't have an auto setting, bring the dish up to the correct temperature in a pan before transferring to the slow cooker as it contains raw chicken. Cook on low for 6–8 hours, or for a faster meal, turn to high for 4 hours. Add the fresh coriander 20 minutes before serving, reserving a little to sprinkle on each bowl. Allow to cool before freezing.

4   To serve, garnish with the remaining coriander and a dollop of natural yoghurt or crème fraîche.

Pea and Ham Soup

A quick and easy soup that is really tasty – perfect for a delicious lunch or supper.

PLAN AHEAD
Hob recipe
Double up
and freeze

Serves 4

200g frozen peas	300ml milk
1 onion, finely chopped	2 sticks of finely chopped celery
25g butter	8 mint leaves
1 dessertspoon of olive oil	Seasoning to taste
150g chopped cooked ham	2 tbsp crème fraîche
300ml hot vegetable stock	

1   Remove the frozen peas from the freezer so they start to defrost at room temperature.

2   Place the chopped onion, butter and olive oil in a saucepan and cook on a medium heat until the onion starts to soften. The olive oil helps to prevent the butter from burning.

3   Add the ham and cook for another 3–5 minutes.

4   Add the hot stock, milk, frozen peas, celery, mint leaves and seasoning. Cover with a lid and cook for another 10–15 minutes.

5   Remove from heat. Add the crème fraîche and liquidise the soup using an electric stick blender. Check the seasoning before serving. Allow to cool before freezing.

Red Pepper and Tomato Soup
with a Pesto Swirl

You can use tinned tomatoes in this, if you prefer, though it does change the taste of the soup. Try both and see which you prefer. If using tinned tomatoes, add two teaspoons of sun-dried tomato paste to boost the flavour.

PLAN AHEAD
Hob recipe
Double up
and freeze

Serves 4

Spray of olive oil

1 large onion, chopped

1–2 garlic cloves crushed

4 red peppers, deseeded and chopped

½ tsp chilli powder

4–6 fresh tomatoes, skinned and chopped

1 tsp paprika

1 litre of water (or low-salt vegetable stock)

Black pepper to taste

Pesto (fresh or jar) to serve

1   Cook the onion, garlic and peppers together in a pan with a spray of olive oil until soft and the onions are translucent. Add the chilli powder and stir well.

2   Add the tomatoes and cook for 2 minutes. Then add the paprika and water or stock and cook slowly on a low heat for 1 hour.

3   Cool slightly, then use an electric stick blender to blitz the soup until it is smooth. Add black pepper to taste and reheat when you are ready to serve. Allow to cool before freezing.

4   Ladle the soup into bowls and add a spoonful of pesto to the centre of each one. Using a sharp knife, swirl the pesto from the centre of the bowl.

Squash Soup with Spiced Yoghurt

I love this soup. The spiced yoghurt really adds to the flavour. It's a perfect autumn soup, making use of the cheap squash on offer.

PLAN AHEAD
Hob recipe
Double up
and freeze

Serves 4–6

Spray of olive oil

1 red onion, diced

1–2 garlic cloves, crushed

1 tsp coriander seeds

1 butternut squash, diced

1 tsp ground coriander

1–2 heaped tsp curry powder

1 cooking apple, diced

400–500ml water or low-salt vegetable stock

Seasoning to taste

200g 0-per cent fat natural Greek yoghurt to serve

1 chilli, deseeded and finely chopped to serve

1 tsp hot paprika to serve

1   Sauté onions, garlic and coriander seeds in a light spray of olive oil for 3–4 minutes to help soften.

2   Add the butternut squash, ground coriander and curry powder and cook for further 3–4 minutes.

3   Add the apple and then the water or stock. Put a lid on and cook on low/medium heat for 30 minutes, until the apple and squash are tender.

4   Season to taste before liquidising, using an electric stick blender to save on washing up. Allow to cool before freezing.

5   In a separate bowl, mix the yoghurt, chilli and paprika together.

6   To serve, place the soup in bowls and add a dollop of yoghurt in the centre.

Minestrone Soup

A lovely wholesome soup. When preparing this, try to keep the vegetables all to a similar size – not only does this ensure they cook more evenly, they also look much better when you serve it.

PLAN AHEAD
Slow cooker recipe
Double up
and freeze

Serves 4

1 red onion, chopped

1–2 garlic cloves, crushed

1 carrot, diced

1 red pepper, deseeded and finely chopped

1 celery stick, finely chopped

3–4 fresh tomatoes, skinned and chopped

50g tinned red kidney beans, drained

50g fresh green beans, chopped

500ml low-salt vegetable stock

3 tsp tomato purée

½ tsp of cayenne pepper

1 tsp paprika

2 bay leaves

Seasoning to taste

50g cabbage, shredded

50g dried spaghetti, broken into small pieces

Small handful of fresh basil, roughly chopped

1   If your slow cooker needs to be preheated, turn it on 15 minutes before using. Refer to your manufacturer's instructions for more information on your specific model temperatures.

2   Add all the ingredients except the cabbage, spaghetti and basil. Make sure the stock is hot when adding as this will help to bring the soup up to temperature quickly.

3   Turn your slow cooker to low for 6–8 hours or, if you want a faster meal, turn to high for 4–5 hours.

4   Twenty minutes before serving add the shredded cabbage, dried spaghetti and basil. Allow to cool before freezing.

Leftover Tip

This is a great soup to use up any vegetables that might be lurking at the bottom of your fridge.

Bubble and Squeak Patties

This is a great dish for using up any leftovers, and whether you serve it hot or cold, it is addictive and delicious.

PLAN AHEAD
Grill or hob recipe
Packed lunches and picnics
Double up
and freeze

Serves 4–6

500g leftover potatoes (can be mashed or roast)

400g leftover greens

Half a bunch of spring onions, finely chopped

100g feta cheese

6 slices of bacon or pancetta, finely chopped

1 tsp wholegrain mustard

Seasoning to taste

1   Place the potatoes and greens in a bowl. Add the spring onions, feta cheese, bacon or pancetta and wholegrain mustard, mash or combine thoroughly. This is much easier with mashed potato, but if you have leftover roast potatoes, you could heat them slightly in the microwave or on the hob before mashing as it helps to make them more pliable. Season to taste.

2   Form the mixture into small patties. Don't worry if they are lumpy, as this is part of their charm. Freeze before cooking.

3   Grill or fry the patties on both sides until golden and serve as a side dish with any leftover roast meat.

Traditional Cornish Pasties

If I am planning on making pastry, I normally spend a whole afternoon bulk baking and fill up the freezer with a variety of pastry goods. Double up this recipe and freeze the pasties before cooking. Remember, the golden rule to always fill your oven, so you can pop in some ready-made pasties from the freezer when you are cooking other meals.

PLAN AHEAD
Oven-cook recipe
Packed lunches and picnics
Double up
and freeze

Serves 4

150g plain flour	350g lean rump steak
75g butter, chilled	1 tsp paprika
1 onion	1 tsp mixed herbs (optional)
1 carrot	Seasoning to taste
1 potato	Beaten egg for glazing
100g swede	

1   Start by making the pastry. Place the flour in a large bowl and add small pieces of the chilled butter. Using your fingertips, rub the butter into the flour until the whole mix resembles breadcrumbs. Add 5–6 tablespoons of cold water (a little at a time) and mix until it forms a dough. Wrap the dough in clingfilm and place in the fridge to cool for 15–20 minutes.

2   Preheat the oven temperature to 200°C (gas mark 6) if you are going to bake the pasties at once.

3   Chop the vegetables and steak into small dice, place in a bowl and mix thoroughly. Add the paprika and herbs; season well.

4   Roll the pastry out onto a floured surface until even and large enough to cut out four circles. Use a small round plate approximately 20cm in diameter as a template.

5   Place some of the steak and vegetable mix in the centre of each circle
    – do not overfill. Use beaten egg or water to brush the edges of the
    pastry before bringing the edges together and crimping until sealed.
    If freezing, freeze before baking.

6   Place the pasties on a lined baking tray. Brush with beaten egg and
    bake for 15 minutes until the pastry starts to turn golden. Reduce the
    heat to 160°C (gas mark 3) and cook for a further 30–35 minutes.

Top Tip

*May be frozen cooked or uncooked. If heating from frozen, add
10 minutes to the cooking time. The food is ready when it is
piping hot throughout. Check and if it is not ready, pop back
into the oven for another five minutes, then check again.*

Sausage in a Blanket

This is a traditional favourite for Christmas lunch to accompany
the turkey, but why wait until then? Serve these with mash and
vegetables for a variation on sausage and mash, or simply enjoy
as a snack for a packed lunch or picnic.

PLAN AHEAD

**Oven-cook recipe
Packed lunches and picnics
Double up
and freeze**

Serves 4

8–10 rashers of lean bacon	Rosemary sprigs
6–8 good-quality sausages	Olive oil

1   Preheat the oven to 200°C (gas mark 6).

2   Wrap some bacon around each sausage, with a sprig of rosemary tucked inside each parcel, and place on a greased or non-stick baking tray, seam side down. Freeze before cooking.

3   Drizzle with a little olive oil and place in the oven for 15–20 minutes until cooked, turning the sausage rolls occasionally.

Corned Beef and Potato Tart

This is a really old family recipe, but it never fails. It always goes down well with hungry children and men!

PLAN AHEAD
Oven-cook recipe
Packed lunches and picnics
Double up
and freeze

Serves 4

100g plain flour	1 onion, diced
50g chilled butter	1–2 tsp Worcestershire sauce
350g of tinned corned beef	1 egg, beaten
3–4 potatoes, cooked and mashed (you can use leftover mash for this)	Seasoning to taste
	Beaten egg for glazing

1   Make the pastry by placing the flour in a large bowl and add small pieces of the chilled butter. Using your fingertips, rub the butter into the flour until the whole mix resembles breadcrumbs. Add 5–6 tablespoons of cold water (a little at a time) and mix until it forms a dough. Wrap the dough in clingfilm and place in the fridge to cool for 15–20 minutes.

2   Preheat your oven to 200°C (gas mark 6).

3   Place the corned beef, mashed potato and diced onion in a bowl and mix thoroughly. Add the Worcestershire sauce and beaten egg and season well.

4   Roll the pastry out onto a floured surface until even. Line a 24cm pie
     dish and trim away the excess pastry. Place a piece of baking parch-
     ment over the pastry, cover with baking beans and blind bake in the
     oven for 15 minutes.

5   Remove the baking beans and parchment and add the corned beef
     mix. You can cover the pie with a pastry lid or, for a fancy look, use a
     lattice top made from strips of pastry. Finish by brushing with beaten
     egg. If freezing, freeze before baking.

6   Place back in the oven and bake for 25 minutes.

Top Tip

*The food is ready when it is piping hot throughout. Check and
if it is not ready, pop back in the oven for another five minutes,
then check again.*

Extra Recipes

*These also taste good if you use puff pastry and make **Little
Corned Beef and Potato Patties** – ideal for the lunchbox.
Simply roll out your puff pastry and with an 8cm cutter cut
out circles. Place a spoonful of the corned beef mixture in the
centre of each circle of pastry, brush the edges with beaten egg
and place another circle of pastry on top. Press down or crimp
the edges. Bake in a hot oven (200°C, gas mark 6) for 15–20
minutes until golden.*

Homemade Pizza

To save time, you could make your own dough in advance. Roll it out and place each piece on greased foil or a baking parchment sheet. Stack the pizza bases on top of each other, cover in clingfilm or foil and refrigerate for up to 2 days or freeze for up to 3 months.

PLAN AHEAD
Oven-cook recipe
Packed lunches and picnics
Double up
and freeze

Serves 4–6

Basic Dough Recipe	325ml warm water
7g dried yeast	1 tsp brown sugar
500g strong bread flour	2 tbsp olive oil

1   Sift the flour into a bowl.
2   Mix the water, yeast, sugar and oil together, making sure that the sugar is dissolved. Make a well in the middle of the flour and pour in the wet mixture.
3   Mix thoroughly, before transferring the dough onto a floured board. Knead well until the dough springs back when pulled.
4   Place the dough in a floured bowl and cover with clingfilm or a warm, damp cloth until doubled in size (or 'proved'). This takes about 1 hour.
5   Knead the dough again, and divide into individual portions, or as preferred. This dough can be stored in the fridge or freezer until needed.

Basic Pizza Topping

Pizza topping can be made using pasta sauce or even simple tomato purée mixed with olive oil and herbs. There are no hard and fast rules for pizza toppings so experiment with whatever you fancy and have fun. Below are some suggestions to help you but, really anything goes!

Tomato and cheese

Pepperoni, mushrooms, red onions and cheese

Ham and mushroom

Ham, pineapple and cheese

Chorizo, jalapenos, tomato and cheese

Red onions, black olives, tomatoes, cheese and red peppers

Roasted vegetables

Baking the Pizza

1   Preheat your oven to 200°C (gas mark 6).

2   Once your dough has proved, roll it out on a floured surface to the desired thickness and size. Cover with your toppings, starting with the tomato base.

3   You can place the pizza on a tray or lay it on a sheet of foil and place directly on the top rack in the oven. Cook for 12–18 minutes until golden.

4   Serve with a green salad and **Homemade Potato Wedges** (page 61).

Storage Tip

Freeze pizza bases ready to top. Prepare and roll them out as above and freeze with baking parchment between each base. Your family can then remove the frozen base from the freezer, add their their favourite topping and place it in the oven for 15–20 minutes.

Cheese and Potato Puffs

When I was a teenager, these were served in our school canteen.
I loved them with plenty of tomato ketchup!

PLAN AHEAD
Oven-cook recipe
Packed lunches and picnics
Double up
and freeze

Serves 4–6

3–4 potatoes, cooked and
mashed (or use leftover mash)

1 onion, diced

1 carrot, grated

150g mature Cheddar, grated

3 eggs, beaten (2 for filling, 1 for
glaze)

½ tsp paprika

Pinch of cayenne pepper
(optional)

1 pack of ready-rolled puff pastry
or half a 500g block

Flour for rolling out

Seasoning to taste

1   Cook and mash the potatoes and preheat the oven to 200°C (gas
mark 6).

2   Place the potatoes, diced onion, grated carrot and cheese in a bowl and
mix thoroughly. Add 2 of the beaten eggs and spices; season well.

3   Roll the pastry out onto a floured surface to 3mm thick and cut into
10-cm squares.

4   Place some of the cheese and potato mixture in the centre of each
square – do not overfill. Use the remaining beaten egg to brush
the edges of the pastry before bringing the edges together to form
a triangle. Crimp to seal the edges. This item can be frozen before
cooking, if you wish.

5   Place the pastries on a baking tray lined with baking parchment.
Brush with beaten egg and bake in the oven for 20–25 minutes, until
the pastry is golden and flaky.

Sun-dried Tomato and Goats' Cheese Frittata

This is an ideal dish for using up leftover cheese. You can use goats' cheese, or why not try some blue cheese for a different flavour. I always have a jar of sun-dried tomatoes in my store cupboard. They last for ages and adding a couple can really transform a dish.

PLAN AHEAD

Oven-cook recipe
Packed lunches and picnics
Packed lunches
and picnics

Serves 4

5 eggs, beaten	4–6 sun-dried tomatoes, chopped
4–5 spring onions, finely chopped	1 tsp mixed herbs
120g goats' cheese, crumbled	Seasoning to taste

1 Preheat your oven to 200°C (gas mark 6).

2 Crack the eggs into a large bowl and beat well. Add the remaining ingredients and combine.

3 Thoroughly grease a 24-cm ovenproof dish before pouring in the mixture.

4 Bake for 20–25 minutes until the frittata is firm, then serve hot or cold with salad.

--- **Leftover Tip** ---

*No sun-dried tomatoes? Instead, make **Vegetable Frittata** by replacing the tomatoes with left-over vegetables.*

Spinach and Feta Filo Pie

This is the perfect dish for a summer evening!

Serves 4–6

40g butter	Finely grated nutmeg to taste
220g pack of filo pastry	Seasoning to taste
400g baby leaf spinach, roughly torn	50g mature Cheddar, grated (optional)
300g feta cheese, crumbled	Sesame seeds
2 eggs, beaten	

1　Preheat your oven to 200°C (gas mark 6).

2　Melt the butter in a saucepan or microwave, keeping a close eye on it to make sure it does not burn.

3　Layer 4–5 sheets of filo pastry in the base of a 24-cm pie dish. Brush melted butter between the sheets and allow the sheets to hang over the edge to give you enough to form the sides of the pie.

4　Place the spinach in a colander, and rinse with hot water until it starts to wilt. Place this in a mixing bowl. Add the feta, beaten eggs and nutmeg; season well. (If you like a cheesy dish, add 50g of grated mature Cheddar.) Once mixed, transfer the filling to the pastry base.

5　Bring the edges together to form a crust or rough topping. Brush with butter, then scrunch up more filo sheets and place these in the gaps, brushing with butter to cover all the pastry. If freezing, freeze before baking.

6　Finish with a sprinkling of sesame seeds, then place in the oven and bake for 25–30 minutes, until crisp and golden. Serve hot or cold with a green salad and baby new potatoes.

Sausage and Herb En Croute

Mum would sometimes add to this a layer of pickle or sliced tomato, especially if she had any soft ones to use up. Delicious!

Serves 6–8

Flour for rolling out	1 onion, chopped
500g puff pastry	2–3 tsp mixed herbs
500g quality lean sausage meat	1 egg, beaten

1 Preheat the oven to 200°C (gas mark 6).

2 On a floured surface, roll the pastry out to around 4mm thick, into a 30cm square.

3 Mix the sausage meat, chopped onion and herbs together in a bowl.

4 Spread the sausage meat down the centre of the pastry, allowing at least 8–10cm of pastry either side of the meat and about 3–4cm at the base.

5 Brush the egg over the exposed pastry – you will use this pastry to fold over the sausage meat.

6 Using a sharp knife, cut the remaining pastry at a slight diagonal into 2–3cm strips (stopping about 3cm away from the sausage meat). Fold these strips, alternating from one side of the sausage meat to the other, over the sausage meat to form a pleated pattern.

7 Ensure the pastry is secure and all the sausage meat is covered. If freezing, freeze uncooked and defrost before cooking. Brush with any remaining egg before baking in the oven for 30–40 minutes until golden. Serve hot or cold.

Quiche Lorraine

Whether for a picnic, a Sunday tea or a buffet, a quiche is ideal.

PLAN AHEAD
Oven-cook recipe
Packed lunches and picnics
Double up
and freeze

Serves 4–6

100g plain flour
50g chilled butter
200ml milk
3 eggs
½ tsp mustard powder
A pinch of cayenne pepper

150g Gruyère cheese, grated (use mature Cheddar as an alternative, if you prefer)
1 small onion, finely chopped
75g cooked ham or lean bacon, diced
Seasoning to taste

1   Make the pastry by placing the flour in a large bowl and adding small pieces of the chilled butter. Using your fingertips, rub the butter into the flour until the whole mix resembles breadcrumbs. Add 5–6 tablespoons of cold water (a little at a time) and mix until it forms a dough. Wrap the dough in clingfilm and place in the fridge to cool for 15–20 minutes.

2   Preheat the oven to 200°C (gas mark 6). Roll out the pastry on a floured surface to line a 23-cm greased flan tin. Place a sheet of baking parchment over the pastry and cover with baking beans.

3   Blind bake the pastry case in the oven for 10 minutes. Remove the beans and parchment and cook for a further 5–10 minutes, until the pastry starts to colour slightly. Remove the pastry case from the oven and turn the oven down to 180°C (gas mark 4).

4   Meanwhile, whisk the milk and eggs together thoroughly before adding the mustard powder and a tiny dash of cayenne pepper. Add the cheese, onion and ham or bacon. Season well before pouring into the pastry case. If freezing, freeze before baking.

5   Bake in the oven for 30–40 minutes until golden and the centre is firm. Leave for a few minutes to firm up before serving.

Top Tip

May be frozen cooked or uncooked. If heating from frozen, add 10 minutes to the cooking time. The food is ready when it is piping hot throughout. .

Leftover Tip

*If using cooked ham, see **Ham Hock** recipe on pages 94–95.*

Mediterranean-style Tortilla

This is an ideal dish for using up any leftover vegetables.

PLAN AHEAD
Oven-cook recipe
Packed lunches and picnics
Double up
and freeze

Serves 4

5 eggs, beaten

1 bunch of spring onions, finely chopped

1–2 red peppers, deseeded, diced or thinly sliced

6 rashers of pancetta, diced

3–4 sun-dried tomatoes, chopped

50g Parmesan cheese, grated

Small handful of chopped fresh herbs such as basil, oregano or thyme

Seasoning to taste

1   Preheat your oven to 200°C (gas mark 6).

2   Crack the eggs into a large bowl and beat well. Add the remaining ingredients and combine.

3   Grease a 24-cm ovenproof dish before pouring in the mixture.

4   Bake for 20–25 minutes, until the tortilla is firm. Serve hot or cold with salad.

Puffed Sausage Rolls

Puff pastry is a busy cook's best friend. I spend an afternoon with a couple of packs of puff pastry and fill the freezer with uncooked pastry goods. This really helps, especially at Christmas or when you are entertaining.

PLAN AHEAD

Oven-cook recipe
Packed lunches and picnics
Double up
and freeze

Serves 4–6

500g sausage meat

Flour for rolling out

1 ready rolled pack of puff pastry, or half a 500g block

Beaten egg to glaze

A sprinkle of sesame seeds (optional)

1   Preheat your oven to 200°C (gas mark 6).

2   Roll the sausage meat into lengths about as thick as your thumb.

3   On a floured surface, roll the pastry out to the desired size and thickness. It should be just over twice as wide as your roll of sausage meat, and 1cm longer at each end.

4   Place the sausage mix 1–2cm from the long edge of the pastry. Coat the edges of the pastry with beaten egg, then fold it over the sausage meat.

5   Press down firmly on the edge of the pastry to seal the join, then cut the sausage rolls to the desired length. If freezing, freeze before cooking.

6   Place the sausage rolls on a baking tray, brush with beaten egg and sprinkle with sesame seeds before placing in the oven for 25 minutes, until golden brown.

Top Tip

May be frozen cooked or uncooked. If heating from frozen, add 10 minutes to the cooking time. The food is ready when it is piping hot throughout. Check and if it is not ready, pop back into the oven for another five minutes, then check again.

Storage Tip

I place the sausage rolls on a baking tray and freeze for 2-3 hours before placing the sausage rolls into a freezer bag – this prevents the individual rolls from sticking together.

Extra Recipes

Mix some herbs with the sausage meat to create delicious **Herby Sausage Rolls**. *If you like it hot, mix your sausage meat with freshly chopped chilli and a good dash of Tabasco sauce to create tempting* **Hot, Hot, Hot Sausage Rolls**. *Vegetarians can opt for any of the above by using vegetarian sausage mix. My mum's favourite is to spread pickle or chutney onto the sausage meat – mango chutney is her favourite but any soft pickle will work.*

Cheese Scones

This is a foolproof recipe for light, fluffy and tasty scones.

PLAN AHEAD

Oven-cook recipe
Packed lunches and picnics
Double up
and freeze

Makes 6–8 scones

250g self-raising flour	50g butter
Pinch of cayenne pepper	75g mature Cheddar, grated
1 tsp mustard powder	100ml buttermilk
Seasoning to taste	1 egg (plus 1 beaten egg for glazing)

1   Preheat your oven to 200°C (gas mark 6).

2   Sift the flour into a bowl and add the cayenne, mustard and seasoning.

3   Add the butter and rub in to form breadcrumbs. Add most of the grated cheese and combine well.

4   In a jug, mix the buttermilk with the egg. Gradually add this mixture to the dry ingredients to form a dough that is firm, but not wet.

5   Place the dough on a floured board, and press out with your hands until 3–4cm thick (try not to overwork the dough). Cut out individual scones with a pastry cutter and place on a greased or lined baking tray.

6   Brush the scones with beaten egg and crumble a little grated cheese over the top, if liked.

7   Place in the oven for 15–20 minutes depending on your oven and the size of the scones. Bake until golden.

8   Place on a cooling rack or serve warm.

Top Tip

May be frozen cooked or uncooked. If heating uncooked from frozen, add 5 minutes to the cooking time. These will be ready when they are piping hot throughout, so check and if they are not ready, put back into the oven for another minute or so, then check again. If heating previously cooked scones from frozen, just allow to defrost normally or reheat in an oven for a few minutes.

Storage Tip

Freeze the unbaked scones, then bake from frozen in 15 minutes. If frozen baked, just allow to defrost and re-heat in a few minutes.

Top Tip

Do you have a food processor? Cut the time of preparation by adding the flour, butter, mustard powder, cayenne, seasoning and cheese then whizz! Mix the buttermilk with the egg and then pour this into the processor. Whizz again to form a dough.

Extra Recipes

*Add a little finely chopped onion for **Cheese and Onion Scones**, or some chopped cooked bacon or pancetta for a delicious **Savoury Scone**. Experiment by adding your favourite herbs.*

Tofu and Spinach Quiche

This quiche is one of my favourites. It's a big hit with meat eaters as well as vegetarians – most don't realise they are eating tofu! It's also very simple to make and there's no risk of a soggy, eggy middle that some quiche recipes can suffer from.

PLAN AHEAD

Oven-cook recipe
Packed lunches and picnics
Double up
and freeze

Serves 4–6

100g plain flour	75g mature Cheddar, grated
50g chilled butter	1 onion, finely chopped
400g tofu (not silken)	Dash of finely grated nutmeg
1 bag of baby leaf spinach (approx. 80–100g)	Seasoning to taste

Top Tip

Adapt this for vegans by replacing the Cheddar cheese with vegan cheese or 2 tbsp nutritional yeast flakes.

1   Make the pastry. Place the flour in a large bowl and add small pieces of the chilled butter. Using your fingertips, rub the butter into the flour until the whole mix resembles breadcrumbs.

2   Add 5–6 tablespoons of cold water (a little at a time) and mix until it forms a dough. Wrap the dough in clingfilm and place in the fridge to cool until needed.

3   Preheat the oven to 200°C (gas mark 6).

4   Roll the pastry out onto a floured surface to the correct size and thickness to line a 23-cm greased flan tin. Place a sheet of baking parchment over the pastry and cover with baking beans.

5   Blind bake the pastry case in the oven for 10 minutes. Remove the baking beans and parchment and cook for a further 10 minutes until the pastry starts to colour. Remove the pastry case from the oven and turn the oven down to 180°C (gas mark 4).

6   Meanwhile, mash the tofu thoroughly. Place the spinach in a colander and rinse well with hot water until it starts to wilt. Stir it into the tofu and add the grated cheese, onion and nutmeg. If the mixture is too dry, add a dash of milk and mix well. Season well before pouring into the pastry case. If freezing, freeze before baking.

7   Bake in the oven for 20 minutes until golden. Leave for a few minutes before serving.

Top Tip

May be frozen cooked or uncooked. If heating from frozen, add 10 minutes to the cooking time. The food is ready when it is piping hot throughout. Check and if it is not ready, pop back into the oven for another five minutes, then check again.

Cheese and Spring Onion Quiche

I love this quiche with some rocket and balsamic vinegar!

PLAN AHEAD
Oven-cook recipe
Packed lunches and picnics
Double up
and freeze

Serves 4–6

100g plain flour

50g chilled butter

200ml milk

4 eggs, beaten

100g mature Cheddar, grated

1 bunch spring onions, chopped

Seasoning to taste

1   Preheat the oven to 200°C (gas mark 6).

2   Make the pastry. Place the flour in a large bowl and add small pieces of the chilled butter. Using your fingertips, rub the butter into the flour until the whole mix resembles breadcrumbs.

3   Add 5–6 tablespoons of cold water (a little at a time) and mix until it forms a dough. Wrap the dough in clingfilm and place in the fridge to cool until needed.

4   Roll the pastry out onto a floured surface and use to line your 25-cm flan tin. Put a sheet of baking parchment over the pastry and fill with baking beans.

5   Blind bake for 10 minutes. Remove the baking beans and parchment, and cook for further 10 minutes until the pastry starts to colour. Turn the oven down to 180°C (gas mark 4).

6   Meanwhile, mix the milk and eggs together thoroughly. Add the grated cheese and spring onions, including the green stalks, and mix. Season well before pouring into the pastry case.

7   Bake for 30–40 minutes, until golden and serve with salad.

─── Top Tip ───

Freeze this in its raw state before baking (i.e. after filling the flan case), then bake from frozen for 40-50 minutes.

Goats' Cheese and Red Onion Tarts

These are delicious cold, or warm straight from the oven. May be frozen cooked or uncooked. If heating from frozen, add 10 minutes to the cooking time. The food is ready when it is piping hot throughout. Check and if it is not ready, pop back into the oven for another five minutes, then check again.

PLAN AHEAD
Oven-cook recipe
Packed lunches and picnics
Double up
and freeze

Serves 6–8

1 large red onion, thinly sliced
Oil for frying
100g plain flour
50g chilled butter

2–3 tbsp red onion marmalade
125g goats' cheese, crumbled
Black pepper

1 Preheat the oven to 200°C (gas mark 6).
2 Place the onion in a pan with a little oil and cook until soft.
3 Make the pastry (see **Cheese and Spring Onion Quiche**), then roll it out to 3–4mm thickness and use to line individual tart cases, or one large flan case.
4 Fill the pastry cases with red onion marmalade, followed by a few red onion slices, the crumbled goats' cheese and add black pepper.
5 Bake in the oven for 15–20 minutes until golden, and serve with salad.

Cheese and Vegetable Pasties

Double up on pastry and bake a batch of these vegetarian pasties
alongside some **Traditional Cornish Pasties** (pages 36–7).

PLAN AHEAD

Oven-cook recipe
Packed lunches and picnics
Double up
and freeze

Serves 4–6

100g plain flour (I like to use wholemeal or granary flour)	100g mature Cheddar, grated
	2 eggs
50g chilled butter	1 tsp paprika
1 onion	1 tsp mixed herbs (optional)
1 carrot	Seasoning to taste
1 potato	Beaten egg or milk for glazing
75g swede	

1   Preheat the oven to 200°C (gas mark 6).

2   Make the pastry. Place the flour in a large bowl and add small pieces
    of the butter. Using your fingertips, rub the butter into the flour until
    the mix resembles breadcrumbs.

3   Add 5–6 tablespoons of cold water (a little at a time) and mix until it
    forms a dough. Wrap the dough in clingfilm and place in the fridge
    to cool until needed.

4   Meanwhile, chop the vegetables into small dice. Place them in a
    bowl, add the cheese and eggs and mix thoroughly. Add the paprika
    and herbs, and season well.

5   Roll the pastry out onto a floured surface until even. Using a small,
    round plate approximately 20cm in diameter as a template, cut
    4–6 circles.

6   Place a little of the vegetable mix in the centre of each circle – do not overfill. Use beaten egg or milk to brush the edges of the pastry before bringing them together and crimping until sealed.

7   Place the pasties on a baking tray lined with parchment paper. If freezing, freeze before cooking. Brush with beaten egg before placing in the oven. Bake for 15 minutes until the pastry starts to turn golden. Turn the oven down to 160°C (gas mark 3) and bake for another 30 minutes.

Top Tip

May be frozen cooked or uncooked. If heating from frozen, add 10 minutes to the cooking time. The food is ready when it is piping hot throughout. Check and if it is not ready, pop back into the oven for another five minutes, then check again.

Mozzarella and Cherry Tomato Tarts

These take mere minutes to prepare and look much more impressive than they really are. You can make either one large tart, or several individual ones. For this recipe I have made six individual tarts.

PLAN AHEAD
Oven-cook recipe
Packed lunches and picnics
Double up
and freeze

Serves 6

375g pack ready-rolled puff pastry	Basil leaves
Flour for rolling out	8–10 cherry tomatoes
1 pack of mozzarella	Black pepper

1 Preheat the oven to 200°C (gas mark 6).

2 On a floured surface, roll the puff pastry out to 3–5mm thickness. Cut it into six squares and carefully score a line 1cm in from the edges around each square (do not cut through the pastry – you just want to make a slight indent).

3 Place pieces of mozzarella and a few basil leaves on each pastry square. Add a few cherry tomatoes, halved or whole depending on preference.

4 Season with black pepper, then either freeze before cooking or bake in the oven until the pastry is golden – approximately 15 minutes.

5 Garnish with extra basil leaves before serving.

Top Tip

If freezing, freeze uncooked, then cook from frozen, adding 5-10 minutes to the cooking time given above.

Extra Recipes

Try some alternative toppings for these little tarts.

Pizza Puffs Prepare the pastry as in the recipe then spread a layer of pasta sauce or tomato purée over the pastry square (avoiding the 1cm edge). Add pizza topping ingredients, such as onion, peppers and finish with cheese. Bake in the oven for 15 minutes and serve hot.

Roasted Vegetables and Feta Tart Roll the pastry out for one large tart, then roll the edges inwards to form a crust. Place roasted vegetables and squares of feta cheese in the centre of the tart, garnish with fresh herbs and bake for 20–25 minutes.

Goats' Cheese, Pesto and Cherry Tomato Tart

A really simple quiche that always looks professional

PLAN AHEAD

Oven-cook recipe
Packed lunches and picnics
Double up
and freeze

Serves 4–6

200g granary or malted flour	Seasoning to taste
100g chilled butter	125g goats' cheese, sliced or crumbled
200g crème fraîche	
3 eggs, beaten	150g cherry tomatoes
3–4 tsp pesto	

1 Preheat your oven to 200°C (gas mark 6).

2 Make the pastry. Put the flour in a large bowl and add small pieces of the butter. Using your fingertips, rub the butter into the flour until the whole mix resembles breadcrumbs.

3 Add 5–6 tablespoons of cold water (a little at a time) and mix until it forms a dough. Wrap in clingfilm and cool in the fridge.

4 Roll the pastry out onto a floured surface and use to line a 25cm flan tin. Put baking parchment over the pastry and fill with baking beans.

5 Blind bake in the oven for 10 minutes. Remove the baking beans and parchment and cook for a further 10 minutes, until the pastry starts to colour. Turn the oven down to 180°C (gas mark 4).

6 Meanwhile, make the filling by mixing the crème fraîche, beaten eggs, pesto and seasoning together well. Leave to one side.

7 Place the goats' cheese and cherry tomatoes in the bottom of the pastry dish. Pour over the crème fraîche mix.

8 Bake for 30-40 minutes, until golden, and serve with salad.

Homemade Potato Wedges

These are tasty as an accompaniment to a range of dishes (for example, **Chicken Burgers** on page 76 and **Homemade Pizza** on page 40). Alternatively, you can enjoy them as a quick snack on their own. If you are watching the calories, use spray oil instead of olive oil.

PLAN AHEAD
Oven-cook recipe

Serves 4

3–4 large potatoes	1–2 garlic cloves
1–2 tablespoons of olive oil	½ tsp of mixed herbs
1 teaspoon of paprika	½ teaspoon of chilli

1   Peel and slice the potatoes into wedges. Rinse them in running water, then place in a bowl.

2   Add the olive oil, paprika, chilli, garlic and mixed herbs to the bowl, making sure that you coat the potato wedges well with the oil and spices.

3   Place the potato wedges on a greaseproof oven tray and cook at 200°C for 25–35 minutes, depending on size of the wedges.

4   Turn the wedges occasionally during cooking to prevent them from sticking and to get a more even cook.

Healthy Tip

Make your own spray oil by buying a clean spray container from your local pharmacist and filling it with olive oil.

Tomato, Lentil and Carrot Soup

This soup is a firm family favourite – packed with nutrients, including protein from the lentils.

PLAN AHEAD
Hob recipe
Double up
and freeze

Serves 4–6

1 large red onion, diced

2 garlic cloves

2 tsp paprika

6–8 tomatoes, skinned and chopped

2 carrots, chopped

125g lentils, rinsed

1 tbsp tomato purée

½ red pepper, deseeded and chopped

1 bay leaf

570ml water or low-salt vegetable stock

1 tsp dried basil or a bunch of fresh basil, chopped, to serve

1   Cook the onion, garlic and paprika together in a saucepan until soft and the onions are translucent. Add the remaining vegetables and add to the pan with the bay leaf.

2   Cover the vegetables with water or stock, then place on low heat and cook slowly for 30 minutes.

3   Cool slightly, remove the bay leaf, then purée the soup with an electric stick blender and reheat gently when ready to serve. Allow to cool thoroughly before freezing.

4   Serve garnished with dried or chopped fresh basil.

POULTRY

The majority of the recipes in this chapter feature chicken, but you can substitute turkey in most with very little difference in flavour. Turkey has less fat than chicken so is the healthier option.

Always remember the golden rule: if you are turning on your oven, fill it up! So, if you are making a roast or oven dish for a main meal, refer back to the list of oven-cook recipes at the end of this book (pages 257–59) for some quick and easy savouries you can cook at the same time for the week ahead. Some can be prepared in advance and others can be frozen, so double up the recipe and freeze one as a delicious and nutritious, homemade ready meal.

When you cook chicken in a slow cooker, always add hot stock, or warm a sauce *before* adding it to the raw meat, or cook the chicken quickly in a pan; this will help to bring the food up to cooking temperature quickly, reducing the risk of bacterial growth.

Simple Chicken Curry

You can't beat a good, homemade curry. Forget the high-fat, high-salt jars of sauce, this recipe uses your own, homemade paste. Simply store in the fridge in an airtight container, or freeze until needed.

PLAN AHEAD
Slow cooker recipe
Double up
and freeze

Serves 4

3cm piece of fresh ginger, peeled

3–4 garlic cloves

1–3 chillies, deseeded, depending on personal taste and strength

1 stalk of lemon grass, peeled

1–2 tbsp olive oil

Small handful of fresh coriander leaves

1 tbsp garam masala

6 fresh tomatoes, skinned

1 large onion, chopped

1 pepper, deseeded and sliced

1–2 sweet potatoes, diced

50g red lentils

400g chicken breasts, diced

200ml low-fat coconut milk

3 tbsp 0 per cent fat Greek yoghurt

Zest of 1 lime

Rice to serve

1   In a food processor, place the ginger, garlic, chilli, lemon grass, olive oil, coriander, garam masala and tomatoes, reserving some coriander to add just before serving. Whizz until you form a paste, then leave this to one side to rest. You can do this ahead of time and store the paste in the fridge or freeze until needed.

2   Cut the vegetables and chicken into equal-sized pieces so that they cook evenly. Remove the skin and any visible fat from the chicken.

3   If your slow cooker needs to be preheated, turn it on 15 minutes before using. Refer to the manufacturer's instructions for more information on your specific model temperatures.

4   Place all the ingredients apart from the Greek yoghurt and lime into the slow cooker. If the curry looks too thick, add a little water.

5   Cook on low for 6–8 hours or, for a faster meal, turn to high for 3–4 hours. Twenty to thirty minutes before serving, stir in the Greek yoghurt, the chopped coriander saved from earlier and the lime zest. Serve on a bed of rice.

6   If freezing, cook, then allow to cool thoroughly before freezing in individual family portions.

Hearty Chicken Casserole

This is a great standby to use up any leftovers, whether chicken or vegetables, and makes a warming, wholesome meal.

PLAN AHEAD
Slow cooker recipe
Double up
and freeze

Serves 4–6

1 red onion, finely chopped

1–2 garlic cloves, crushed

2 sticks of celery, chopped

1 large leek, chopped

1 large carrot, diced

1 large potato, diced

1 large sweet potato, diced

400g tin of tomatoes (or 4–6 ripe, fresh tomatoes)

400g chicken pieces (thighs, legs or breasts)

100g lardons (optional)

75g red lentils

700ml chicken stock

2 tsp paprika

1 bay leaf

1   If your slow cooker needs to be preheated, turn it on 15 minutes before using. Refer to the manufacturer's instructions for more information on your specific model temperatures.

2   Put all the ingredients in the slow cooker. Make sure the stock is hot when you add it, as this will help the casserole to quickly get up to temperature.

3   Turn your slow cooker to low and cook for 6–8 hours, or if you want a faster meal, turn to high for 4–5 hours. Serve with jacket potatoes.

4   Allow to cool thoroughly before freezing in individual family portions.

Extra Recipes

*Add **Herb Dumplings** (page 103), or create a pie with a simple pastry top. Or make a lovely soup by reusing half of the casserole and liquidizing it.*

Healthy Tip

Add red lentils to increase the nutritional value as well as help to thicken the stock. You could also swap the red lentils for a dried-soup mix, if preferred.

Spring Chicken Casserole

This is the perfect dish to make use of those lovely spring vege-tables. Spring can be a bit chilly so try this delicious, warming meal.

PLAN AHEAD
Hob recipe
Double up
and freeze

Serves 4

Spray of olive oil	2 tsp paprika
400g chicken breasts	Black pepper
250g new potatoes, finely sliced	Small handful of fresh tarragon
1 carrot, finely diced	Small handful of fresh parsley
Bunch of spring onions, chopped	50g French beans
450ml warm chicken stock	75g peas

1   Spray a sauté pan with olive oil. Add the chicken and cook until it starts to brown. Add the sliced potatoes, carrot and spring onions and cook for another 5 minutes.

2   Add the stock, seasoning and herbs. Cover and simmer gently for 15 minutes.

3   Add the French beans and peas and cook for another 15 minutes.

4   Serve with sweet potato mash for a warming supper.

5   Allow to cool completely before freezing in individual or family portions – don't forget to label and date!

Cooking Tip

Use frozen peas direct from the freezer, if you wish.

Cajun Chicken Casserole

Cajun spice for a casserole with some zing!

PLAN AHEAD

Slow cooker recipe
Double up
and freeze

Serves 4–6

1 onion

2–3 garlic cloves, crushed

1 chilli, deseeded and finely chopped

2–3 tsp Cajun spice

1 tsp paprika

1 Red pepper, deseeded and sliced

400g chicken pieces (thigh, legs or breast)

2 sticks of celery, diced

400g tin of chopped tomatoes

1   If your slow cooker needs to be preheated, turn it on 15 minutes before using. Refer to your manufacturer's instructions for more information on your specific model temperatures.

2   Add all the ingredients, making sure the stock is hot when adding as this will keep the temperature high.

3   Turn your slow cooker to low and cook for 6–8 hours, or if you want a faster meal, turn to high for 4–5 hours.

Top Tip

Once cooked, allow to cool before freezing in single or family portions. Label and date. Defrost thoroughly before reheating.

Moroccan-style Chicken and Vegetable Tagine

I love using spices to create new dishes. This dish uses a lot of spices, but allow them to infuse and the taste is amazing. If you don't like things too hot, you can omit the chilli.

PLAN AHEAD
Slow cooker recipe
Double up
and freeze

Serves 4

400g–450g chicken breasts, diced (or equivalent quantity of thigh or leg meat)

3–4 tbsp olive oil

2.5cm pieces of fresh ginger, finely chopped

1 tsp paprika

1 tsp cumin

1 tsp turmeric

1 tsp cinnamon

1 chilli, deseeded and finely diced

Small handful of fresh mint leaves

Small handful of coriander leaves

1 tin of chopped tomatoes

1 large onion, sliced

2 garlic cloves, roughly chopped

1 green pepper, deseeded and thickly diced

2 sweet potatoes, cut into chunks

1 carrot, diced

60g green beans

400g tin of chickpeas, drained

300–400ml chicken stock

1   Chop the chicken into chunks and place in a bowl.

2   In a food processor, blitz together 2 tablespoons of the olive oil, the ginger, spices, chilli, half the chopped fresh herbs and the tomatoes to form a marinade.

3   Pour the marinade over the chicken and cover with clingfilm. Then leave to marinate overnight or for at least 2 hours.

4 If your slow cooker needs to be preheated, turn it on 15 minutes before using. Refer to your manufacturer's instructions for more information on your specific model temperatures.

5 Place a little olive oil in your sauté pan set over a medium heat. Add the onion, garlic and pepper; cook for 3–5 minutes before adding the chicken, holding back most of the marinade until you add the remaining ingredients.

6 Cook for 5 minutes before adding all the other ingredients, including the marinade.

7 Simmer gently for 5 minutes, then add the remaining herbs and transfer to the slow cooker.

8 Cook on low for 4–6 hours. Serve with cous cous.

Top Tip

Once cooked, allow to cool before freezing in single or family portions. Label and date. Defrost thoroughly before reheating.

Chicken, Bacon and Bean Casserole

This wholesome dish is perfect to fill a gap, especially on a dark winter's evening. The beans and lentils provide an extra protein boost, helping to bulk out the casserole and keep you feeling full for longer. As it is quite a substantial meal in itself, you don't need to serve it with anything else.

PLAN AHEAD
Hob recipe
Double up
and freeze

Serves 4–6

Olive oil spray

1 red onion, finely chopped

3 garlic cloves, roughly chopped

1 pepper, deseeded and diced

400g lean, skinless chicken pieces (thigh gives more flavour)

4–5 rashers of lean back bacon, trimmed of all fat

8 new potatoes, halved or quartered

1 large sweet potato, diced

2 carrots, diced

2 sticks of celery, diced

400g tin of chopped tomatoes

900ml chicken stock

75g red lentils

400g tin borlotti beans (or chickpeas)

2 tsp paprika

1 bay leaf

Black pepper

1 tsp dried tarragon

1   In a sauté pan, add a spritz of oil. Heat through and then add the onion, garlic and pepper. Fry for 5 minutes.

2   Add the chicken and fry until it turns white, turning, before adding the bacon.

3   Add all the remaining ingredients, place on a low heat, cover and simmer for 1¼ hours.

--- **Top Tip** ---

Once cooked, allow to cool before freezing in single or family portions. Label and date. Defrost thoroughly before reheating

--- **Leftover Tip** ---

*Double up this recipe and turn half into a **Chicken Hotpot**. Simply add some sliced potatoes to the top with a sprinkling of grated cheese. Bake in the oven at 190°C (gas mark 5) for 20–25 minutes until golden and bubbling.*

Cheat's Chicken and Vegetable Curry

Such an easy dish! No messing about with herbs and spices, as you can use a jar. Simply chop and go! The beans, lentils and vegetables add to the nutritional value.

PLAN AHEAD
Slow cooker recipe
**Double up
and freeze**

Serves 4–6

3–4 chicken breasts	50g red lentils
1 large red onion, finely chopped	400g tin of chickpeas, drained
1 pepper, deseeded	420–500g jar of curry sauce (I use Balti)
2 sweet potatoes	
1 white potato	150g spinach

1 If your slow cooker needs to be preheated, turn it on 15 minutes before using. Refer to your manufacturer's instructions for more information on your specific model temperatures.

2 Remove any visible fat from the chicken and dice evenly. Prepare the pepper and potatoes and dice evenly, too, in pieces roughly the same size as the chicken.

3 Place the chicken and vegetables in the slow cooker, then add the lentils and chickpeas.

4 Pour the curry sauce into a small pan, half-fill the jar with water and shake, then add to the sauce and heat gently, before pouring into the slow cooker.

5 If you do have an automatic setting on your slow cooker, pour the curry sauce and water straight in and switch the setting to auto. The cooker will start at a high temperature, then automatically switch to low for the remainder of the cooking time.

6 Cook on auto or low for 8–10 hours.

7 Twenty minutes before the end of the cooking time, add the spinach and start to cook rice to accompany the curry, if you wish. Serve with mango chutney and naan bread.

Top Tip

Once cooked, allow to cool before freezing in single or family portions. Label and date. Defrost thoroughly before reheating.

Cooking Tip

If you don't have an automatic setting on your slow cooker, it is a good idea to heat up the liquid before you add it, as this will speed up the heating time and minimise any of the potential food poisoning risks associated with slow-cooking poultry.

Leftover Tip

This is a great recipe to use up any cooked chicken left over from a roast. Just add the chicken in the last hour of the cooking time, as it is already cooked.

Chicken Burgers

These are a great favourite with teens. Batch-cook, and they can have a ready supply in the freezer for when they're starving! Much healthier than processed frozen burgers or fast food outlets. Remember to use your frozen breadcrumbs made from stale bread (page 12).

PLAN AHEAD
Hob recipe
Double up
and freeze

Serves 4

1 onion, chopped

1–2 garlic cloves, crushed

1 stick of celery, chopped

½ yellow pepper, deseeded and chopped

500g chicken or turkey mince

30g pine nuts

1 tbsp home-prepared wholemeal breadcrumbs (page 21)

1 egg, beaten (if needed)

1   Place all the ingredients apart from the egg in a food processor and blend thoroughly.

2   When mixed, form into balls – these should be firm but moist. If the mixture is dry, add some beaten egg.

3   Use the palm of your hand to flatten the balls into burger shapes. You can place these in the fridge until you are ready to use them, or freeze them (see tip box, opposite).

4   When you are ready to cook the burgers, you can grill, oven-cook or fry them, just as you would with shop-bought, processed burgers.

5   Serve in wholemeal baps, with a salad garnish, **Homemade Potato Wedges** (page 61) and a dollop of mayonnaise.

Storage Tip

Place the burgers in a single layer on a baking tray to freeze. Once frozen, you can bag them and they won't stick together. If you don't have room to freeze them on a tray, layer between squares of baking parchment to prevent them from freezing into one huge lump. Defrost each burger thoroughly before cooking on a low heat until piping hot.

Healthy Tip

Try turkey mince for an even healthier alternative to chicken.

Cheat's Leftover Chicken Pie

This is my mum's recipe. Now we have grown up and flown the nest, Mum and Dad have had to adapt to cooking for two instead of four. This meal is made from the leftovers of the Sunday roast, so they usually tuck into it early in the week.

PLAN AHEAD
Oven-cook recipe
Double up
and freeze

Serves 4–6

A drizzle or spray of olive oil

1 onion, chopped

2 sticks of celery, chopped

75g mushrooms, quartered

200–300g cooked chicken

100g cooked ham (optional)

295g can chicken or mushroom condensed soup

Flour for rolling out

250g ready-made puff pastry

Little milk for glazing

1   Preheat your oven to 200°C (gas mark 6).

2   Heat the oil and fry the onion in a pan until it starts to soften. Add the celery, mushrooms, cooked chicken and ham (if using). Cook for 3–4 minutes.

3   Stir in the soup and heat for a further 3 minutes. Then pour the mixture in a deep, ovenproof 20cm pie dish.

4   On a floured surface, roll out your pastry larger than required. Wet the edges of the dish with milk or water, then cut thin strips of pastry to place on the edge of the pie dish, all the way round. Dampen these pastry strips with milk to give the top pastry something to hold onto. Cut the top pastry to size and place over the pie. Crimp and seal the edges thoroughly. (If freezing, freeze before baking). Glaze with milk.

5   Bake for 30 minutes, until the pie crust is golden.

6   Serve with new potatoes and salad.

Top Tip

Once cooked, allow to cool before freezing in single or family portions. Label and date. Defrost thoroughly before reheating.

Coq au Vin

This quick and easy variation on the traditional French favourite, is a delicious midweek supper dish to share with friends.

PLAN AHEAD
Slow cooker recipe
Double up
and freeze

Serves 4

500g chicken (thigh gives the best flavour)

12 shallots

3–4 garlic cloves, thickly sliced

80g button mushrooms

2 tbsp plain flour

1 tsp paprika

black pepper

Olive oil

200g smoked lardons

250ml red wine

200ml port

350ml hot chicken stock

2 bay leaves

2–3 sprigs of thyme

1   Cut the chicken into large pieces, then peel and slice the shallots and garlic. Halve or quarter the mushrooms.

2   If your slow cooker needs to be preheated, turn it on 15 minutes before using. Refer to the manufacturer's instructions for more information on your specific model temperatures.

3   In a bowl, mix together the flour, paprika and black pepper.

4   Heat a little olive oil in a sauté pan, then toss the chicken pieces in the flour and add them to the pan. Add the lardons and cook a little until the chicken starts to brown. Remove from the heat.

5   Add all the ingredients to the slow cooker. Make sure the stock is hot, as this will help to keep the temperature high.

6   Turn your slow cooker to auto and cook for 8–10 hours or, if you want a faster meal, turn to high for 5–6 hours.

7   Check the casserole 30 minutes before the end of the cooking time.

8   Remove the bay leaves before serving with sauté or mashed potatoes
     and green vegetables.

Top Tip

*Once cooked, allow to cool before freezing in single or family
portions. Label and date. Defrost thoroughly before reheating.*

Cooking Tip

*When checking the casserole (see Step 7), if the sauce is too
liquid, mix 1–2 tablespoons of cornflour with a little water, pour
this into the stock pot and turn the setting to high for the last
half an hour.*

Chicken and Mushroom Casserole

This family favourite is delicious served with new or mashed potatoes and green vegetables.

PLAN AHEAD
Hob recipe
Double up
and freeze

Serves 4

A drizzle or spray of olive oil	300ml chicken stock
1–2 garlic cloves	1 tsp cornflour
2 leeks, finely chopped	dessert spoonful of water
6 spring onions, finely chopped	1 tsp paprika
300g chicken pieces	100g French beans
175g mushrooms	1 tsp dried tarragon (or a handful
200ml white wine	of fresh tarragon)

1   Heat a little olive oil in a casserole pan and fry the garlic, leeks and spring onions for 2–3 minutes. Add the chicken and the mushrooms and cook for a further 5 minutes.

2   Add the wine and stock to the casserole.

3   Mix the cornflour with the water in a cup to form a smooth paste and add to the casserole.

4   Add all the remaining ingredients. If you are using fresh tarragon, add half now and retain half to add in the last 10 minutes of cooking. Season to taste before popping on the lid.

5   Cook at a low to medium heat for 30–40 minutes.

Top Tip

Once cooked, allow to cool before freezing in single or family portions. Label and date. Defrost thoroughly before reheating.

Leftover Tip

To make this recipe, you can use chicken from your Sunday roast.

Cooking Tip

If you prefer a creamier sauce, stir in 2–3 tablespoons of crème fraîche 5 minutes before serving.

Extra Recipes

Add Herb Dumplings (page 103), or create a pie with a simple pastry top. Or make a lively soup by reusing half of the casserole and liquidizing it.

Tandoori Chicken

If you are short of time, you can always use shop-bought tandoori paste, but this dish is fun to make yourself.

PLAN AHEAD
Oven-cook recipe
Double up
and freeze

Serves 4

1 onion, finely chopped	2–3 tsp paprika
2–3 garlic cloves, crushed	2.5cm piece of fresh ginger, grated
1 tsp coriander powder	
1 tsp cayenne pepper	1–2 chillies, deseeded and finely chopped
1 tsp chilli powder (or fresh chillies, deseeded and finely chopped)	
	Juice and zest of 1 lemon
3 tsp curry powder	2 tbsp olive oil
2 tsp turmeric	250ml Greek yoghurt
	450g large pieces of chicken

1   In a large ovenproof dish, mix the onion, garlic, herbs and spices with the lemon juice, zest, olive oil and yoghurt.

2   Add the chicken pieces and combine thoroughly. For the best flavour, cover with clingfilm and leave to marinate in the fridge for a few hours.

3   When you are ready, preheat your oven 180°C (gas mark 4).

4   Place the chicken and the marinade in an ovenproof dish and cook for 20–25 minutes. Serve on a bed of rice.

Chicken Vindaloo

This is quite a hot dish, so adjust the spices to suit your taste. I normally make several curry dishes, including **Lentil Dahl** (page 163), and serve them together for a selection of flavours and heat.

PLAN AHEAD

Slow cooker recipe
Double up
and freeze

Serves 4

2 tbsp olive oil	2 tomatoes
1 chilli	250ml water or stock
2 garlic cloves	Small handful of fresh coriander leaves
3–4 tbsp vindaloo paste	
1 tsp turmeric	500g chicken fillets, diced
1 tsp ground cumin	1 large onion, diced

1   Place all the ingredients apart from the chicken and onion in the food processor and whizz until a paste forms.

2   Place the chicken in a bowl or freezer bag, pour on the paste and marinate for a few hours. If short of time, you can skip this step.

3   Preheat the slow cooker, following the manufacturer's instructions

4   Put the chicken, paste and onion in the slow cooker. Combine well and cook on high for 4–5 hours, or low for 6 hours.

8   Serve with rice and Indian chutneys.

Top Tip

Once cooked, allow to cool before freezing in single or family portions. Label and date. Defrost thoroughly before reheating.

Spicy Chicken Wings

A really simple dish that takes minutes to prepare. Marinate overnight or for at least one hour before cooking in the oven.

PLAN AHEAD

Oven-cook recipe

Serves 4–6

1–2 chillies, deseeded and finely chopped	1 tsp allspice
2 garlic cloves, finely chopped	½ tsp ginger
2–3 tsp chilli sauce (mild or hot, depending on your taste)	½ tsp chilli powder
	1 tbsp brown sugar
Juice and zest of 1 lemon	2 tsp maple syrup or 3 tsp honey
1 tsp paprika	Seasoning to taste
	10–12 chicken wings

1　In a bowl or large freezer bag, combine all the ingredients apart from the chicken wings. Then add the chicken wings and mix well until they are thoroughly coated. Cover with clingfilm or seal the bag and leave to marinate in the fridge overnight or for at least one hour.

2　When ready to cook, preheat the oven to 200°C (gas mark 6).

3　Tip the wings and the marinade into a baking tray with a lip or an ovenproof dish, and bake for 20 minutes or until the chicken is cooked. Serve with rice and a green salad, or **Homemade Potato Wedges** (page 61).

Cooking Tip

Check that the chicken is cooked thoroughly by pushing a clean skewer into the thickest part of the meat. If red juices emerge, put back into the oven for another five minutes, then check again. The chicken is cooked when the juices run clear.

Sticky Chicken Drumsticks

These can be cooked on the barbecue. A lovely summer treat!

PLAN AHEAD
Grill recipe

Serves 4

6 tbsp maple syrup or honey

2 tbsp mustard

2 tbsp Worcestershire sauce

2 tbsp soy sauce

4 tsp paprika

8 chicken drumsticks

1   Place all the ingredients apart from the chicken in a large freezer bag and mix well.

2   Score the drumsticks with a knife to help the marinade take.

3   Add the chicken to the freezer bag and shake well to ensure it is well coated. Seal the bag and leave the chicken in the fridge to marinate overnight.

4   When you are ready to cook, line your grill tray with foil to collect any mess and heat the grill to its highest setting.

5   Arrange the chicken on the grill tray and place under the heat. Cook the chicken on both sides, basting with the marinade, if you like your chicken really sticky. Grill until the chicken is thoroughly cooked, reducing the heat if the outside appears to be cooking too quickly.

6   Serve with salad and savoury rice, or **Homemade Wedges** (page 61).

Roasted Herby Vegetables and Chicken Breasts

This very easy one-pot meal makes a perfect, satisfying choice after a busy day. To get ahead, prepare the vegetables the night before.

PLAN AHEAD
Oven-cook recipe

Serves 4

600g small new potatoes, washed	3–4 garlic cloves, crushed
1 large sweet potato, cubed	Zest of 1 lemon
1 parsnip, quartered lengthways	400g–450g chicken breasts
2 tsp paprika	1 red onion, quartered
Olive oil	2–3 baby leeks, cut into 3 pieces
Large handful of fresh mixed herbs (such as thyme, rosemary, oregano)	1–2 red peppers, deseeded and thickly sliced
	8–12 small vine tomatoes, whole

1   Preheat your oven to 200°C (gas mark 6). In a large bowl, combine the potatoes, sweet potato and parsnip. Add the paprika and 2 tablespoons of olive oil and combine until well coated.

2   Pour this into an ovenproof dish or tray and add a little more oil if it looks too dry. Bake in the oven for 20 minutes.

3   Finely chop the herbs. Add the crushed garlic, 1–2 tablespoons of olive oil and lemon zest. Combine well.

4   Rub half of this mixture over the chicken breasts and add them to the vegetables in the tray. Add all the remaining ingredients, scatter over the remaining herbs and combine everything well. Add more oil, if necessary.

5   Bake for another 30–35 minutes until the vegetables and chicken are cooked through.

Roasted Squash One-Pot Chicken

I love one-pot meals, because they are so simple. Roasted sweet potato and squash have a fantastic flavour – add some garlic and chilli and you have a divine meal. Feel free to add more chilli to taste, or for extra flavour, use chilli oil instead of olive oil.

PLAN AHEAD
Oven-cook recipe

Serves 4

2 large red onions, cut into wedges

4 garlic cloves, left whole

1–2 chilli, deseeded and finely sliced

3 sweet potatoes, skin on, cut into thick chunks

1 small squash, skin on, cut into chunks

Spray olive oil or chilli oil to drizzle

4 tsp paprika

Black pepper

450g chicken breasts

12 cherry tomatoes

1   Preheat the oven to 200°C (gas mark 6).

2   Arrange the onion, garlic, chilli, sweet potatoes and squash in a roasting tin and spray with oil. Toss well and spray again, if necessary.

3   Sprinkle paprika and pepper over the vegetables and roast for 10 minutes.

4   Add the chicken and cherry tomatoes to the vegetable mixture. Spray again with oil and bake for another 20–25 minutes, until the chicken is cooked.

5   Serve with a green salad.

Chicken Chow Mein

A quick and easy chow mein, and a great way to use up cooked chicken left over from a roast. If you're short of time, use a bag of ready-chopped stir-fry mix – simply add your chicken and the remaining seasonings.

PLAN AHEAD

Hob recipe

Serves 4

400g chicken pieces, thinly sliced

2–3 tsp Chinese five spice

Olive or sesame oil

2.5cm piece of ginger, finely sliced

1 chilli, deseeded and finely sliced

3–4 garlic cloves, crushed

2 carrots, finely chopped into thin slices

4–5 broccoli florets

4–6 spring onions, sliced diagonally

1 pepper, deseeded and sliced

½ small spring cabbage, shredded

Handful of bean sprouts (optional)

50g mushrooms, sliced

300g noodles

3 tbsp sweet dry sherry or rice wine

2–3 tsp soya sauce

Juice of half a lemon

3 tbsp sweet chilli sauce

1   Mix the chicken with the Chinese five spice. If you are using fresh chicken, cook it in wok with a splash of oil for a few minutes until browned, then leave to one side until needed.

2   Pour some more oil in the wok and add the ginger, chilli and garlic. Next, add your chopped vegetables (apart from the bean sprouts and mushrooms) and cook for another 2 minutes, until the vegetables start to wilt slightly, but do not go soft.

3   Add the chicken, bean sprouts, mushrooms and the noodles to the wok. Cook for one more minute.

4   Add the dry sherry or rice wine, soya sauce, lemon juice and sweet chilli sauce. Stir well for one minute before serving immediately.

Homemade Chicken Nuggets

Kids love chicken nuggets and this recipe is really quick and easy so why not ask them to lend a hand? It is also good to know that they are getting fresh chicken in their nuggets, not processed meat.

PLAN AHEAD
Oven-cook recipe
Double up
and freeze

Serves 4

350g–400g skinless and boneless
    chicken fillets

4 tbsp plain flour

3–4 tsp chicken seasoning

2 tsp paprika

2 eggs, beaten

100g breadcrumbs (made from
    your left over bread, page 12)

Olive oil spray

1   Preheat the over to 220°C (gas mark 7).

2   Cut the chicken into nugget-sized pieces.

3   Take three bowls. In the first bowl, mix flour, seasoning and paprika. To the second bowl, add beaten eggs. And in the third bowl, put the breadcrumbs.

4   Dip the chicken into the first bowl, ensuring each nugget is well coated. Then follow into the second bowl, again ensuring all sides are covered. Do the same for the third bowl.

5   Place the chicken nuggets onto a greased baking tray. Spray lightly with oil and bake for 20 minutes until golden.

6   Serve with **Homemade Potato Wedges** (page 61).

— Healthy Tip —

Make your own spray oil by buying a clean spray container from your local pharmacist and filling it with olive oil.

Chicken, Pepper and Tomato Pasta

A simple family favourite that takes less than 30 minutes to prepare.

PLAN AHEAD

Hob recipe

Serves 4

Spray of olive oil

3–4 chicken breasts, cut into chunks

1 small red onion, finely chopped

2–3 garlic cloves, crushed,

1–2 red peppers, deseeded and cut into slices

100g button mushrooms, whole or halved (optional)

400g tin of chopped tomatoes,

2 tbsp sun-dried tomato paste

Small handful of fresh basil leaves, torn

300g whole-wheat or gluten-free penne pasta

1   In a sauté pan, add a spray of olive oil. Add the chicken chunks and cook for 5–8 minutes.

2   Add the onion, garlic, peppers and mushrooms, if using. Cook for 5 more minutes before adding the tomatoes, sun-dried tomato paste, basil leaves and seasoning. Leave on a low heat to simmer gently.

3   Cook the pasta in boiling water according to the packet instructions.

4   Drain the pasta and add to the chicken mixture, stirring well until everything is well combined. Season to taste before serving.

MEAT

Whether you are cooking meat from scratch or using a leftover joint for a meal, there is a huge amount of versatility. The recipes in this chapter are family favourites. Some, such as Beef Stroganoff (page 99), can be made using leftover meat from your Sunday beef joint. You can also mince up the leftover joint meat to make your own mince (pages 124–134) for recipe suggestions). Here, you'll find crowd-pleasers ranging from Toad in the Hole (page 109) right through to casseroles and pasta dishes. Some can be prepared in advance. Some can be frozen, so remember the Busy Mum's Golden rule: double up the recipe and freeze one or turn it into another simple and delicious meal.

Ham Hock

You can use this recipe to cook ham or gammon joints too, but ham hock is a really cheap, tasty meal in its own right, served with a **parsley sauce** (page 159), sauté potatoes and green vegetables.

PLAN AHEAD
Slow cooker recipe
**Double up
and freeze**

Serves 4–8

1 onion, quartered	2–4 ham hocks
1 carrot, roughly chopped	

1   If your slow cooker needs to be preheated, turn it on 15 minutes before using. Refer to your manufacturer's instructions for more information on your specific model temperatures.

2   Place the onion, carrot and ham hocks in the slow cooker. Fill with water until the ham is just covered.

3   Cook on low for 6–8 hours.

4   Remove the hocks. Trim away the skin and slice or flake the ham from the bone. Use as you wish, hot or cold.

Top Tip

Once cooked, allow to cool before freezing in single or family portions. Label and date. Defrost thoroughly before reheating.

Cooking Tip

You should be able to fit 3–4 hocks in your slow cooker, depending on its size. I use water to cook the ham as I have found stock creates a very salty ham. One ham hock should feed two people. Slow-cooked, the outer skin does stay white. You can cut this off, or if you like it crisp, bake the finished ham on the middle shelf of your conventional oven for 30 minutes at 180°C at the end of the cooking time.

Extra Recipes

*If you like a **baked hock**, take the cooked joint and glaze with a drizzle of honey or, if you prefer, you could stud the meat with some cloves. Place in the oven at 190°C (gas mark 5) and bake for 30 minutes or until golden.*

Flake off the meat to use hot or cold: ham hock is perfect in sandwiches, as a filling for a quiche, in soups or simply on its own with egg and chips, or a salad.

Irish Lamb Stew

Speak to your butcher to get the best cuts of meat. Opt for cheaper cuts when slow cooking, as the process helps to tenderise the meat.

PLAN AHEAD
Slow cook recipe
Packed lunches and picnics
Double up
and freeze

Serves 4–6

1 onion, finely chopped	150g bacon or lardons
2 garlic cloves, crushed	½ tsp dried thyme
2 carrots, thickly sliced	1 tsp dried parsley
1 sweet potato, diced	1 bay leaf
2–3 potatoes, thickly diced	200ml white wine
500g lamb	400ml lamb stock

1 If your slow cooker needs to be preheated, turn it on 15 minutes before using. Refer to your manufacturer's instructions for more information on your specific model temperatures.

2 Put all the ingredients in the slow cooker, making sure that the stock is hot, as this will help to get the temperature high quickly.

3 Turn your slow cooker to low and cook for for 8–10 hours.

4 Serve with a garnish of freshly chopped parsley.

Top Tip

Once cooked, allow to cool before freezing in single or family portions. Label and date. Defrost thoroughly before reheating.

Tunisian Lamb

This is a very easy recipe that makes a dinner that is packed full of flavour. The next day, serve any leftovers with warm pitta bread.

PLAN AHEAD
Slow cooker recipe
Double up
and freeze

Serves 4–6

Olive oil

500g lamb, diced

1 large onion, diced

1 large carrot, diced

1 sweet potato, diced

2–3cm piece of fresh ginger, roughly chopped

2 garlic cloves, roughly chopped

2–4 tbsp harissa paste (depending on strength)

1 tsp ground cinnamon

8 olives, halved

8–12 dried apricots

500ml lamb stock

50g flaked almonds

1   If your slow cooker needs to be preheated, turn it on 15 minutes before using. Refer to your manufacturer's instructions for more information on your specific model temperatures.

2   Heat a little olive oil in a sauté pan and add the lamb. Brown the meat, drain off any fat and place the lamb in the slow cooker.

3   Add all the remaining ingredients apart from the flaked almonds.

4   Cook on low for 8–10 hours, then just before serving, stir in the flaked almonds.

5   Serve with couscous.

Top Tip

Once cooked, allow to cool before freezing in single or family portions. Label and date. Defrost thoroughly before reheating.

Lamb Shanks

One of my dad's favourite dishes. This really benefits from a slow cook – you want the lamb to fall off the bone and melt in your mouth.

PLAN AHEAD
Slow cooker recipe
Double up
and freeze

Serves 4–6

2 red onions	400g tin of chopped tomatoes
3 garlic cloves, crushed	300ml red wine
2 sticks celery, finely sliced	3 tsp balsamic vinegar
1 leek, finely sliced	400ml low-salt lamb stock, hot
1 carrot, finely diced	1 bay leaf
1 sweet potato	Sprigs of fresh thyme and
4 lamb shanks (approx. 400g each)	rosemary

1 If your slow cooker needs to be preheated, turn it on 15 minutes before using. Refer to your manufacturer's instructions for more information on your specific model temperatures.

2 Prepare all the vegetables, making sure they are roughly the same size so they cook evenly.

3 Place all the ingredients in the slow cooker. Make sure they are combined well and evenly distributed. Set the slow cooker to low and cook for 8–10 hours, until the lamb is tender.

4 Prior to serving, if your liquid is too thin, stir in 1–2 teaspoons of cornflour, dissolved in a little water, and turn heat up to thicken for 5–10 minutes. Season to taste before serving with mashed potato.

Top Tip

Once cooked, allow to cool before freezing in single or family portions. Label and date. Defrost thoroughly before reheating.

Extra Recipes

Any lamb left? Shred it and fill a warm pitta bread – just add some shredded lettuce, peppers, onion and a dash of chilli sauce. Or add the shredded lamb to a pan of stir-fry vegetables to make a delicious meal in minutes.

Beef Stroganoff

This tasty supper cooks in under 20 minutes – perfect for a busy evening or when you are unexpectedly late home from work.

PLAN AHEAD
Hob recipe

Serves 4

Olive oil	300g button mushrooms
500g beef fillet or tenderloins, cut into very fine strips	2 tsp chopped fresh tarragon (or 1 tsp dried)
2 onions, finely chopped	300ml sour cream
1–2 garlic cloves, crushed	Freshly chopped parsley
15g butter	

1 Place the beef, onion and garlic in a sauté pan with a little olive oil and cook for 3–6 minutes, turning occasionally.

2 Add the butter and mushrooms and cook for another 3–6 minutes, until the mushrooms are tender but not too soft and the onions and beef are cooked.

3 Add the tarragon and sour cream, and season to taste. Allow to simmer very gently for 8–10 minutes.

4 At the end of the cooking time, add some chopped parsley, stir well and serve on a bed of rice.

Wholesome Lamb and Vegetable Casserole

If you are not a fan of lamb, this recipe also works well with chicken. A thick broth liquid with lovely chunky vegetables and meat – you don't need anything else with this dish, except perhaps some bread to mop up the juices!

PLAN AHEAD

Slow cooker recipe
Double up
and freeze

Serves 4–6

1 large onion, diced	75g dried soup mix
2–3 carrots, diced	800ml low-salt chicken, lamb or vegetable stock
1–2 sweet potatoes, diced	
3–4 potatoes, diced	½ tsp dried parsley
500g lamb, trimmed and cut into chunks	1 bay leaf

1   If your slow cooker needs to be preheated, turn it on 15 minutes before using. Refer to your manufacturer's instructions for more information on your specific model temperatures.

2   Chop your vegetables chunky and roughly to the same size so that all the ingredients cook evenly.

3   You can brown the meat first in a frying pan on the hob if you prefer, but I have cooked both browned and added straight to the slow cooker and really can't tell any difference, so now I skip the browning (and the additional washing up) and add all the ingredients together. Make sure the stock is hot when you add it.

4   Cook on low for 8–10 hours.

Top Tip

Once cooked, allow to cool before freezing in single or family portions. Label and date. Defrost thoroughly before reheating.

Healthy Tip

For added nutrition, the recipe includes dried soup mix. You can buy this in most supermarkets alongside the other dried pulses and beans. These mixes normally contain red lentils, split peas, dried peas, barley and aduki beans.

Extra Recipes

*Double up this recipe to make **Lamb Hotpot** in the same batch. Simply transfer the casserole to an oven-proof dish and add some sliced potatoes to the top with a sprinkling of grated cheese. Bake in the oven at 190°C (gas mark 5) for 20–25 minutes until golden and bubbling.*

Beef and Ale Stew with Herb Dumplings

A very traditional recipe and a wholesome dish that will satisfy most appetites. This recipe always tastes nicer the following day, so plan ahead and cook it the day before you want to eat.

PLAN AHEAD
Slow cook recipe
Double up
and freeze

Serves 4–6

For the stew

1–2 tbsp lain flour	1 leek, finely sliced
2–3 tsp paprika	2–3 carrots, sliced
400g beef stewing steak, chunks	1 parsnip, sliced
1–2 tbsp olive oil	125g button mushrooms
1 red onion, finely chopped	1 beef stock cube
1 tbsp redcurrant jelly	1 bay leaf
600ml ale of your choice	

1   If your slow cooker needs to be preheated, turn it on 15 minutes before using. Refer to your manufacturer's instructions for more information on your specific model temperatures.

2   Place 1–2 tablespoons of flour in a bowl and mix in the paprika. Dip in the beef chunks and ensure they are thoroughly coated.

3   Heat the olive oil in the sauté pan. Add the beef and onion; fry until the beef starts to brown.

4   Stir in the redcurrant jelly and, when it has melted, pour in the ale. Heat gently before transferring to the slow cooker.

5   Add all the remaining stew ingredients (not the dumpling mixture), place on low heat and cook for 8–10 hours.

For the dumplings

100g self-raising flour   2–3 tsp mixed herbs

50g suet   4 tbsp water

6   Forty-five minutes before serving, mix the dumpling ingredients
    together in a bowl to form a dough and roll into small balls, roughly
    the size of a walnut.

7   Place these on top of the stew, cover and cook for 30 minutes, until
    the dumplings fluff up.

Top Tip

*Once cooked, allow to cool before freezing in single or family
portions. Label and date. Defrost thoroughly before reheating.*

Extra Recipes

*Double up to make **Beef and Ale Pies**. Remember, if you
are doubling up this recipe, you will need to remove half before
adding the dumplings in step 6. Just pop the stew into your pie
dishes and cover with some puff pastry.*

Spicy Beef and Bean Casserole

This is an ideal recipe for cheaper stewing beef or tougher cuts of beef as the slow cooking helps to tenderise the meat.

PLAN AHEAD
Slow cook recipe
Double up
and freeze

Serves 4–6

1–2 tbsp plain flour

1 tsp ground ginger

Seasoning

400g stewing beef, cut into chunks

1 red onion

2 garlic cloves

1 chilli, deseeded and finely chopped

1 red pepper

1 tin of tomatoes

2 carrots, sliced

1 sweet potato

200g tin of red kidney beans, drained

400g tin of mixed beans, drained

1–2 tsp chilli powder (depending on personal taste)

1 tbsp Worcestershire sauce

50ml red wine vinegar

300ml beef stock

1   If your slow cooker needs to be preheated, turn it on 15 minutes before using.

2   Mix the flour and ground ginger together and season. Toss the beef chunks in the flour until they are evenly coated.

3   Brown the meat in a pan with some olive oil, onion and garlic.

4   Evenly distribute all the ingredients in the slow cooker.

5   Cover and cook slowly for 6–8 hours. Serve with rice or mashed potatoes and steamed vegetables.

Top Tip

Once cooked, allow to cool before freezing in single or family portions. Label and date. Defrost thoroughly before reheating.

Lamb and Green Lentil Curry

The green lentils in this recipe help to bulk out the curry, so you don't need to use as much lamb.

PLAN AHEAD

Slow cook recipe
Double up
and freeze

Serves 4

Olive oil

400g lamb, cut into chunks

1 onion, sliced

2–3 garlic cloves, crushed

2.5cm piece of fresh ginger, sliced

1–2 chillies, deseeded and finely chopped

1 tsp cinnamon powder

1 tbsp medium curry powder

Juice of half a lemon

400g tin of chopped tomatoes

175g green lentils

500ml warm water or warm lamb stock

Small handful fresh chopped coriander

150g low-fat yoghurt or quark

1   If your slow cooker needs to be preheated, turn it on 15 minutes before using. Refer to your manufacturer's instructions for more information on your specific model temperatures.

2   If you wish, start by browning the lamb in a sauté pan, but this is not essential. Then put all the ingredients, apart from half the coriander and the yoghurt or quark, into the slow cooker.

3   Cook on auto for 8–10 hours, until the lamb is tender.

4   Just before serving, stir in the yoghurt and the remaining coriander.

Top Tip

Once cooked, allow to cool before freezing in single or family portions. Label and date. Defrost thoroughly before reheating.

Beef Bourguignon

This recipe is perfect for a dinner party, as you can prepare it in advance and enjoy being a host as it cooks.

PLAN AHEAD
Slow cook recipe
Double up
and freeze

Serves 4

750g beef steak, diced	1 sweet potato, diced
1–2 tbsp plain flour	400g tin of chopped tomatoes
1–2 tbsp olive oil	300ml of red wine (ideally Burgundy)
1 small red onion, diced	
1–2 garlic cloves, chopped	1 tsp dried thyme
200g shallots	2 heaped tsp paprika
150g pancetta, diced	1 beef jellied stock pot
2 carrots, diced	150g button mushrooms

1   If your slow cooker needs to be preheated, turn it on 15 minutes before using.

2   Toss the beef in the flour before adding to a sauté pan with a the olive oil. Cook until the beef has browned, then remove from the pan and place it in your slow cooker.

3   Add all the remaining ingredients and combine well in the stock pot. Place on low and cook for 8–10 hours.

4   Serve with mashed potato and steamed green leafy vegetables.

――― **Top Tip** ―――

Once cooked, allow to cool before freezing in single or family portions. Label and date. Defrost thoroughly before reheating.

Corned Beef Loaf

This is an old-fashioned recipe, but kids really love it, so why not give it a try? It's delicious with **Rich Tomato Sauce** (page 130).

PLAN AHEAD
Oven-cook recipe
Double up
and freeze

Serves 4

4–5 small potatoes, cooked and mashed (or can use leftover)

300g corned beef, mashed

1 onion, finely chopped

2 garlic cloves, crushed (optional)

1–2 tsp wholegrain mustard

2–3 tsp tomato purée

50g wholemeal breadcrumbs (page 12)

1 egg, beaten

Seasoning to taste

1   Place the mashed potato and mashed corned beef in a very large bowl. Add all the remaining ingredients and combine well.

2   Transfer the mixture to a lined 454g loaf tin, pressing down firmly and smoothing out the top.

3   Place in the oven and bake for 25 minutes at 180°C (gas mark 4).

4   Leave to cool for five minutes before turning out onto a serving dish. Can be served hot or cold, in slices, with **Rich Tomato Sauce** (page 130).

— Storage Tip —

If you know you are going to freeze the meat loaf, line the tin with greased clingfilm before adding the loaf mixture. Place in the freezer in the loaf tin until frozen. Remove the frozen loaf from the tin, wrap well in baking parchment and then foil. Place in a freezer bag back in the freezer until you need it. Cook at 180°C (gas mark 4) for 35 minutes.

Roasted Cherry Tomato, Pancetta and Ricotta Pasta

You really can't beat pasta meals when you are in a hurry and just fancy something filling and delicious. This is one of my favourite dishes – it's quick and easy, but very tasty.

PLAN AHEAD
Oven-cook recipe

Serves 4

4 tbsp olive oil	330g cherry tomatoes
1 small red onion, quartered	1 tsp dried thyme
4 garlic cloves, sliced	1 tsp dried oregano
Half a red pepper, deseeded and sliced	300g dried penne pasta
	125g ricotta (half a tub)
4–5 rashers of pancetta or lean bacon	1 bunch of fresh basil leaves, torn
	Seasoning to taste

1   Preheat the oven to 200°C (gas mark 6).

2   Place the onion, garlic, pepper, pancetta and cherry tomatoes in a roasting dish with the olive oil and dried herbs. Mix thoroughly to ensure everything is covered in oil. Bake for 10–15 minutes, turning occasionally.

3   Meanwhile, cook the pasta in boiling, salted water according to the packet instructions.

4   Drain the pasta and combine with the tomato mixture in the roasting dish. Stir in the ricotta and basil and season to taste.

5   Serve immediately in the dish.

Toad in the Hole

This is a classic family favourite, but do try to invest in some good-quality sausages, as these really do improve the flavour. If you are busy, you can prepare the batter the day before, and leave it in a jug in the fridge.

PLAN AHEAD
Oven-cook recipe
Double up
and freeze

Serves 4–6

100g plain flour

300ml milk

1 egg

1 onion, chopped

8 lean sausages

Olive oil

A handful of fresh herbs such as thyme, oregano or rosemary (or 2 tsp dried herbs)

Seasoning to taste

1   Preheat your oven to 200°C (gas mark 6).

2   Using a blender with a balloon whisk attachment, blend the flour, milk and egg together to form a batter. Mix thoroughly and leave to settle.

3   Meanwhile place the onion, sausages and a drizzle of olive oil in a deep ovenproof dish. Place in the oven for 15 minutes, turning occasionally.

4   Just before the 15 minutes is up, give the batter mix a quick whizz with your balloon whisk, adding the herbs and seasoning before a final whisk.

5   Remove the sausages from the oven and immediately pour over the batter, ensuring that all the sausages are covered.

6   Return to the oven and bake for 20–25 minutes until golden.

7   Serve with onion gravy and steamed vegetables.

Storage Tip

If freezing, cook the sausages thoroughly and allow to cool before adding the batter. Divide into individual or family portions before freezing. Bake from frozen for 30-35 minutes at 220°C (gas mark 7).

Leftover Tip

*Double up the batter and pour it into small tin foil cases (the size that fits in a cupcake tray). They will be ready to pop in the oven to make your own **Yorkshire Puddings** next time you are making a roast. These will keep for keep months uncooked in the freezer.*

Sausage Casserole

This is a really hearty dish, perfect for autumn evenings. If you wish, you can use beef, but I prefer a good-quality pork sausage, sometimes with chilli to add a bit of a kick.

PLAN AHEAD
Hob recipe

Serves 4

454g pack of lean, good quality sausages, left whole

4–6 rashers of bacon or lardons, chopped

1 large red onion, sliced

Olive oil

2 garlic cloves, crushed

2 red peppers, deseeded and finely sliced

2 sweet potatoes, diced

400g tin of chopped tomatoes

175ml red wine

2 tsp paprika

Small handful of fresh chopped parsley

1   Place the sausages, bacon and onion in a large sauté pan or casserole dish suitable for use on the hob. Drizzle with olive oil and cook over a medium to high heat until the sausages are browned and the onion has softened.

2   Put all the remaining ingredients in a casserole dish and season to taste.

3   Cook over a low to medium heat at a slow simmer for 20 minutes until the vegetables are soft.

4   Serve with mashed or jacket potatoes.

Top Tip

While you cook the sausages, double up and brown some ready for **Toad in the Hole** *(page 109).*

Stuffed Loin of Pork

A great family roast, served with roast potatoes, vegetables and home-made gravy. Remember, if you have the oven on, fill it up.

PLAN AHEAD
Oven-cook recipe

Serves 4–6

75g breadcrumbs (page 12)

1 red onion, finely chopped

2–3 garlic cloves, finely chopped

150g lean bacon, chopped

50g pine nuts

6–8 sun-dried tomatoes (in oil), chopped

Handful of fresh herbs, chopped (sage, thyme, oregano or parsley)

Seasoning to taste

1kg loin of pork

Olive oil

Sea salt

1   Preheat your oven to 200°C (gas mark 6).

2   In a mixing bowl, place the breadcrumbs, onion, garlic, bacon, pine nuts, sun-dried tomatoes and chopped herbs. Combine well and season with salt and pepper.

3   Flatten out the meat by bashing it with a wooden rolling pin or tender-iser until flat. Place the stuffing down the centre, then roll tightly. Use water-soaked string to tie the loin securely.

4   Rub the skin with olive oil and sprinkle with sea salt and black pepper.

5   Place the pork on a baking or roasting tray and place in the oven. Cook for 20 minutes before turning down the temperature to 180°C (gas mark 4) and cook for 30 minutes for every 500g in weight. If the pork starts to darken too much while cooking, you can cover securely with tin foil.

6   Use a meat thermometer to check if the meat is cooked, or check the

juices – if they are running clear when you stick a skewer or sharp knife into the meat, it should be cooked.

7 Remove from the oven and cover loosely with foil. Leave to rest for 10–15 minutes before carving.

Top Tip

If you buy your meat from your local butcher, he or she will prepare your stuffed loin for you.

Leftover Tip

Any leftover pork can be used to make up pies or pasties, or you can shred it and add it to vegetable soups. You can also shred the meat and add it to warm pitta breads covered in a chilli sauce for a quick snack.

Ham and Leek Cheesy Bake

This is a comforting supper dish but try not to use shop-bought ham. Instead make your own using the slow cooker (**see Ham Hock**, pages 94–95).

PLAN AHEAD
Oven-cook recipe
**Double up
and freeze**

Serves 4

4 leeks, trimmed

25g butter

1 tbsp plain flour or cornflour

500–750ml milk

2 tbsp nutritional yeast flakes (optional)

75g mature Cheddar cheese, grated

½ tsp mustard powder

Black pepper to taste

8 slices of lean ham or bacon

2–3 tbsp home-prepared whole-meal breadcrumbs (page 12)

2 tbsp oats

25g Parmesan cheese

1   Cut the leeks into 10cm lengths and steam for 5–8 minutes, until just tender. Preheat the oven to 220°C (gas mark 7).

2   While the leeks are steaming, melt the butter gently in a saucepan over a medium heat. Add the flour or cornflour and stir well with a wooden spoon. Add the milk, a little at a time, continuing to stir to avoid any lumps.

3   Switch to using a balloon whisk and continue to stir over a medium heat until the sauce begins to thicken. The balloon whisk will help to eradicate any lumps that may have formed. Add more milk as necessary to get the desired thickness. The sauce should be the consistency of custard.

4   If you are using nutritional yeast flakes, add these next as they will reduce the amount of cheese you may need – taste as you add the cheese to get the flavour right. Add the cheese and mustard, and stir well. Season with black pepper.

5   Remove the leeks from the steamer and wrap a slice of ham or
    bacon around each one. Lay them in the base of an ovenproof dish –
    lasagne dishes are ideal for this.

6   Pour over the cheese sauce. Combine the breadcrumbs, oats and
    Parmesan cheese, sprinkle over the leeks and bake for 20 minutes
    until golden and bubbling.

Top Tip

*Freeze before baking. May be cooked from frozen. Add 10
minutes to cooking time.*

Sweet and Sour Pork

Forget those jars of sweet and sour sauce, this is a really easy
recipe for you to create your own version with none of the artificial colourings or additives.

PLAN AHEAD

Hob recipe

Serves 4

2 tsp sesame oil

2 tbsp light soy sauce

2 tbsp rice wine or white wine
vinegar

2 tbsp tomato purée

1 tbsp brown sugar

400g tin of pineapple chunks in
natural juice

2 tsp cornflour

150ml chicken stock

400g pork, trimmed and cubed

2 garlic cloves, crushed

2 peppers, deseeded and sliced

1–2 inch piece of fresh ginger,
thinly sliced

6 spring onions, sliced

1 teaspoon olive oil

1   Place the sesame oil, soy sauce, vinegar, tomato purée, brown sugar, pineapple chunks and juice, cornflour and stock in a large bowl. Mix until thoroughly combined.

2   Stir-fry the pork cubes in a wok or sauté pan for 5 minutes, until they are coloured.

3   Add the garlic, peppers, ginger and spring onions to the pan and stir-fry for another 5 minutes.

4   Pour over the prepared sauce and continue to cook for another 2–3 minutes.

5   Serve on a bed of rice or noodles.

Bacon and Mushroom Pasta

The perfect quick supper! I prefer to use smoked bacon as I love the flavour, but it is a personal choice. If you are watching your fat intake, you can opt for a low-fat cream cheese or substitute half the quantity with Greek yoghurt or quark for an even healthier variation.

PLAN AHEAD
Hob recipe

Serves 4

300g penne or tagliatelle dried pasta

Olive oil

1 large onion, finely chopped

1–2 garlic cloves, crushed

4–6 rashers of lean bacon, finely chopped

100g button mushrooms

150g cream cheese

2 tbsp milk

Small handful of mixed fresh herbs such as basil, oregano and thyme (alternatively, add 1–2 teaspoons dry or frozen herbs if out of season)

1   Place the pasta in a pan of boiling water and cook following the packet instructions.

2   Meanwhile, in a large sauté pan fry the onion and garlic in a little olive oil for a couple of minutes until the onion starts to soften. Add the bacon and fry for further 5 minutes before adding the mushrooms to the pan.

3   Add the cream cheese, milk and herbs and stir thoroughly.

4   Drain the pasta, and return it to the saucepan. Add the bacon mixture and mix well over the heat of the hob that was used for boiling the pasta for one minute.

5   Season to taste and serve immediately.

Bacon, Leek and Macaroni Cheese Bake

Don't make the cheese sauce for this overly thick – it should be a
nice, thick but flowing sauce that will give your 'mac'n cheese' a
silky-smooth, comforting texture.

PLAN AHEAD
Oven-cook recipe
**Double up
and freeze**

Serves 4

175g macaroni

2–3 leeks, finely chopped

6–8 rashers of bacon, roughly
chopped

Olive oil or butter for frying

25g butter

1 tbsp plain flour or cornflour

500–750ml milk

2 tbsp nutritional yeast flakes
(optional)

75g mature Cheddar cheese

½ tsp mustard powder

Black pepper to taste

2–3 tbsp home-prepared wholemeal breadcrumbs (page 12)

2 tbsp oats

25g Parmesan cheese

1   Preheat the oven to 190°C (gas mark 5). Place the macaroni in boiling,
    salted water and cook until tender. The time will depend on what type
    of macaroni you use, so refer to the instructions on the packet.

2   While the pasta is cooking, gently fry your leeks and bacon in a little
    olive oil or butter. Once cooked, leave to one side.

3   Meanwhile, melt 25g butter gently in a saucepan over medium heat.
    Add the flour or cornflour and stir well with a wooden spoon. Add
    the milk, a little at a time, continuing to stir to avoid lumps.

4   Switch to using a balloon whisk and continue to stir over a medium
    heat until the sauce begins to thicken. The balloon whisk will help
    to eradicate any lumps that may have materialised. Add more milk
    as necessary to get the desired thickness. The sauce should be the
    consistency of custard.

5   If you are using nutritional yeast flakes, add these next as they will
    reduce the amount of cheese you may need – taste as you add the
    cheese to get the flavour right. Then add the cheese and mustard,
    and stir well. Season with black pepper.

6   Drain the macaroni and combine this with the bacon, leeks and
    cheese sauce. Season to taste and pour into an ovenproof dish.

7   Combine the breadcrumbs, oats and Parmesan cheese and sprinkle
    over the bake. At this point you can freeze, once cooled.

8   Place on a low rack in the oven and cook for 15 minutes until golden
    and bubbling.

Top Tip

*Freeze before baking. May be cooked from frozen. Add 10
minutes to cooking time.*

Cooking Tip

*Don't overcook the macaroni when you plan to freeze it, as this
stops it from going a bit rubbery. However, if you reheat very
slowly on a low heat in a saucepan, adding some more milk, it
should be fine.*

Leftover Tip

*This recipe is great for using up any leftover cheese. Grate
oddments of cheese into freezer-proof containers and freeze,
ready to make cheese sauces at a later date.*

Healthy Beef Curry

You can make this curry recipe with vegetables, lamb or chicken.
This uses beef, which works really well in the slow cooker.

PLAN AHEAD

Slow cooker recipe
**Double up
and freeze**

Serves 4

3cm piece of fresh ginger, peeled	½ tsp olive oil
3–4 garlic cloves	500g beef, diced
1–3 chillies, depending on strength and personal taste, deseeded	1 large red onion, chopped (or 2 medium)
1–2 tbsp olive oil	1 pepper, deseeded and sliced
Small handful fresh coriander leaves	400g tin of chopped tomatoes
	200ml water
1 tbsp garam masala	3 tbsp 0-per cent fat Greek yoghurt
½ tsp cumin	
2 tsp turmeric	Zest of 1 lime

1   In a food processor, blend the ginger, garlic, chilli, olive oil, half the coriander leaves, garam masala, cumin and turmeric to a paste. Leave to one side to rest, or store in the fridge or freezer until needed.

2   If your slow cooker needs to be preheated, turn it on 15 minutes before using. Refer to your manufacturer's instructions for more information on your specific model temperatures.

3   Brown the beef gently in a sauté pan with the olive oil, then transfer to the slow cooker along with all the remaining ingredients apart from the yoghurt, reserved coriander leaves and lime.

4   Turn your slow cooker to low and cook for 8–10 hours.

5   Twenty to thirty minutes before serving, taste the sauce. If you need more spice, you can stir in some more garam masala at this stage.

Chop the remaining coriander. Add the Greek yoghurt, chopped coriander and the lime zest.

6   Serve on a bed of rice – ideally brown rice or basmati, if you are health-conscious.

Spicy Moroccan-style Lamb Cutlets

This recipe needs to be marinated for 2–3 hours so plan ahead.

PLAN AHEAD
Grill recipe

Serves 4

100ml pomegranate molasses	2–3 garlic cloves, crushed
Juice and zest of 2 lemons	4 lamb chops
2 tsp chilli powder	4 tbsp Greek yoghurt
2 tsp paprika	Seasoning to taste

1   Combine the molasses, juice and zest of the lemons, chilli, paprika and crushed garlic cloves in a bowl. Season with black pepper.

2   Place the chops in the marinade and leave for 2–3 hours to marinate.

3   When ready to cook, remove the chops from the marinade. In a separate bowl, mix the yoghurt with the marinade then place it in a pan over a very low heat.

4   Place the lamb chops under the grill and grill evenly on both sides, brushing some of the marinade sauce over as you cook.

5   Drizzle the warm marinade over the chops to serve. Serve with cous-cous and salad or, for a more traditional meal, with new potatoes and vegetables.

Quick and Easy Garlic, Mushroom and Ham Tagliatelle

If I am really hungry, I opt for fresh pasta that only takes a couple of minutes to cook. To stop the tagliatelle from getting too sticky on the plate, the secret is to retain a little pasta water (1 or 2 tablespoons) and stir it back into the pasta before serving.

PLAN AHEAD
Hob recipe

Serves 4

350g tagliatelle	Dash of white wine (optional)
Olive oil	Dash of milk
2–4 garlic cloves, crushed	3–4 tbsp low-fat crème fraîche
200g button mushrooms	Grated Parmesan
100g ham, chopped	Handful of fresh parsley, chopped

1   Place the pasta in boiling water and cook following the packet intructions.

2   Meanwhile, heat a little oil in a sauté pan and fry the garlic and mushrooms for 2 minutes. Add the ham and cook for 1 minute.

3   Add a dash of white wine, if using, before adding the milk, crème fraîche and parsley (reserve some to garnish). Stir well.

4   Drain the tagliatelle and stir it into the sauce. Garnish with grated Parmesan and the reserved parsley. Serve immediately.

MINCE

Mince is a terrific, economical ingredient, which can be used to make a variety of family meals. Why not consider buying this in bulk? You can follow the recipes in this section to create batch-cooked recipes, made into single or family portion sizes ready for the freezer, or make a large batch of the base mince recipe on page 124 and store it in 500g portions in your freezer as the base for dozens of different meals. Remember, you can make your own mince from leftover meat from your Sunday joint.

Any of the recipes supplied here can be made by replacing the meat mince with quorn or soy mince to make these meat-free.

Base Mince Recipe

This basic recipe can be used for a multitude of recipes (a few are shown below). My mum makes up these batches but also adds tinned tomatoes and mushrooms. The choice is yours!

PLAN AHEAD
Hob recipe
Double up
and freeze

Serves 4–6

Olive oil

Onions (1 large onion for every 500g of mince)

Garlic (2 garlic cloves, crushed for every 500g of mince)

500g mince

1   Place the oil, onion and garlic in a sauté pan and fry until golden.

2   Drain off any excess fat before adding the mushrooms and tomatoes, if you are using them. Leave to cool

3   Place in freezer-proof containers in either individual or family size portions.

4   Label and freeze when cool.

--- **Top Tip** ---

Use the **Base Mince** in any of the recipes in this chapter. Follow your chosen recipe, omitting any onion or garlic as the base already contains this. Add the base mince when your recipe tells you to add mince and continue as usual.

Moussaka

Traditionally, this recipe uses lamb mince, but to save time, use your prepared **Base Mince** (page 124).

PLAN AHEAD
Oven-cook recipe
Double up
and freeze

Serves 4

2–3 aubergines, cut into slices roughly 5mm thick

Olive oil

1 onion, roughly chopped

2 garlic cloves, crushed

400g lamb mince

400g tin chopped tomatoes

2 tsp tomato purée

1 tsp dried mint

2 tsp cinnamon powder

Seasoning to taste

300ml low-fat crème fraîche

50g mature Cheddar or Parmesan cheese, grated

1 Preheat your oven to 190°C (gas mark 5).

2 Place the aubergines in a pan of boiling water for 2 minutes. Remove and pat dry, then leave to one side.

3 Meanwhile, heat a little olive oil in a sauté pan and fry the onion and garlic. Add the lamb mince and fry until browned.

4 Add the tomatoes, tomato purée, mint, cinnamon and seasoning. Cook for another 2–3 minutes.

5 Place a layer of mince in the base of an ovenproof dish (a lasagne dish is ideal), followed by a layer of aubergine. Continue alternating mince and aubergine, finishing with a layer of mince.

6 Mix the crème fraîche with the grated cheese (reserve a little to garnish) and spread over the final layer of mince. Garnish with a sprinkling of Parmesan. At this point, if you wish to freeze, do so before cooking.

7 Place in the oven and bake for 20–25 minutes, until bubbling and golden on top.

─────────────── **Cooking Tip** ───────────────

If you are using the Base Mince recipe with tomatoes (page 124), you only need to add the herbs and aubergines before following the remaining recipe.

Lasagne

If you are following the **Base Recipe** with tomatoes on page 124, you only need to add herbs before layering the lasagne. For an additional cheat, use a jar of white sauce or a portion made up and frozen at an earlier date to make this the speediest lasagne ever!

PLAN AHEAD
Oven-cook recipe
**Double up
and freeze**

Serves 4

For the Bolognese

A spray of olive oil

1 onion finely chopped

2–3 garlic cloves, finely chopped

1 pepper, deseeded and finely chopped (optional)

400g lean beef mince or vegetarian mince

150ml red wine

75g mushrooms, finely chopped (optional)

3–4 fresh tomatoes, chopped, or 400g tin chopped tomatoes

Mixed herbs to taste

Seasoning to taste

For the white sauce

25g butter

1 tbsp plain flour or cornflour

500ml milk

¼ tsp mustard (optional)

Black pepper to taste

To assemble

6–8 sheets of lasagne (ensure the pack says 'no pre-cooking required')

Grated cheese to garnish

1   Preheat your oven to 190°C (gas mark 5).

2   Fry the onion and garlic in a little olive oil until soft and translucent.
    Add the pepper, if using.

3   Add the mince and cook until brown, followed by the wine and
    mushrooms (if using). Cook for 2 more minutes.

4   Add the fresh or tinned tomatoes and stir well. Finally, add the herbs
    and season to taste. Leave to simmer for 5 minutes.

5   While the Bolognese sauce is simmering, make the white sauce. Melt
    the butter gently in a saucepan over a medium heat. Add the flour or
    cornflour and stir well with a wooden spoon. Add the milk, a little at
    a time, continuing to stir to avoid lumps.

6   Switch to using a balloon whisk and continue to stir over a medium
    heat until the sauce begins to thicken. The balloon whisk will also
    help eradicate any lumps that may have formed. Add more milk as
    necessary to achieve the desired thickness (the sauce should be the
    consistency of custard). Stir in the mustard (if using) and season with
    black pepper.

7   Spoon a layer of Bolognese sauce into the base of your ovenproof la-
    sagne dish and then pour over a thin layer of white sauce. Cover this
    with a layer of lasagne sheets. Repeat the layers, then finish with a
    layer of white sauce. Don't overfill the dish as the lasagne may spill
    out during cooking.

8   Sprinkle grated cheese over the top. At this point you can freeze or
    to cook, place the lasagne in the oven and bake for 35–40 minutes,
    until golden and the pasta sheets are cooked. (The cooking time can
    be greatly reduced if you use fresh lasagne sheets.)

9   Serve with salad and garlic bread.

Top Tip

*Freeze before baking. May be cooked from frozen, or cooked
when defrosted. If cooking from frozen, add 10 minutes to the
cooking time.*

Shepherd's and Cottage Pie

This is a real family favourite. I normally buy a large pack of mince and make up several portions for the weeks ahead. The only real difference between shepherd's pie and cottage pie is the meat. Shepherd's Pie is traditionally made with lamb mince and Cottage Pie with beef. Of course, you can use vegetarian mince if you prefer.

PLAN AHEAD
Oven-cook recipe
Double up
and freeze

Serves 4–6

800g potatoes, cut into rough chunks	1 tsp yeast extract (Marmite or similar)
4 carrots, 2 roughly chopped, 2 cut into small cubes	200ml meat gravy or vegetable gravy, if using vegetarian mince
A spray of olive oil	
1 onion, chopped	Seasoning to taste
400g lean mince (or pre-drained of fat)	Worcestershire sauce
	25g butter
75g mushrooms, sliced (optional)	75g mature Cheddar
100ml red wine	Paprika for sprinkling

1   Preheat your oven to 180°C (gas mark 4).

2   Place the potatoes and the 2 chopped carrots in a steamer. Cook until soft.

3   Meanwhile, heat the oil in a large sauté pan and fry the onion for 1–2 minutes before adding the mince.

4   Cook until brown before adding the cubed carrots, mushrooms (if using) and the wine.

5   Dissolve the yeast extract in the gravy then add to the mince. Cook
    for 15 minutes until the sauce has reduced to the desired consistency.
    Season to taste and add a splash of Worcestershire sauce.

6   Mash the steamed potato and carrots together. Add the butter and
    two thirds of the Cheddar and mix thoroughly.

7   Place the mince in a deep, ovenproof dish and spoon mash over
    the top. Be careful not to overfill the dish. Press the mash down
    gently with a fork, then top with the remaining grated cheese and a
    sprinkling of paprika.

8   Place in the oven and bake for 20–25 minutes. Allow to cool thor-
    oughly, then freeze, if you wish.

Top Tip

*Freeze before baking. May be cooked from frozen, or cooked
when defrosted. If cooking from frozen, add 10 minutes to the
cooking time.*

Spicy Meatballs in Rich Tomato Sauce

Again, this recipe can be used with the **Base Mince** on page 124. Just add herbs and follow the remaining steps below.

PLAN AHEAD
Hob recipe
Double up
and freeze

Serves 4–6

For the meatballs

400g beef mince

1 small onion, finely chopped or grated

1 tsp paprika

1 tsp cumin

1 chilli, deseeded and finely chopped

1 tsp chilli powder

2 tsp Worcestershire sauce

1 tsp parsley

50g breadcrumbs (page 12)

1 egg, beaten

Seasoning to taste

Drizzle of olive oil

For the tomato sauce

400g tin chopped tomatoes (or fresh, skinned and chopped)

2 garlic cloves, crushed

1 tsp sugar

½ tsp salt

Drizzle of olive oil

Handful of fresh, torn basil leaves

Olive oil for frying

1   Combine all the meatball ingredients in a bowl and mix thoroughly.

2   Form the mixture into small balls and place on a baking tray. Cover with a sheet of clingfilm and store in the fridge for 30 minutes to rest, or freeze until needed (see tip opposite).

3   When you are ready to cook, place a little olive oil in a large sauté pan and fry the meatballs gently over a moderate heat until they start to brown.

4 While the meatballs are cooking, make the sauce by combining the
   ingredients for the sauce in a pan and heat gently until they reach a
   mild simmer. Cook for 5-8 minutes before removing from heat..

5 Once the meatballs are browning, add the tomato mixture to the
   sauté pan. Cook for a further 5 minutes, then serve on a bed of
   spaghetti.

Storage Tip

*Freeze the meatballs before cooking. Place them on a baking tray
and freeze for 1 hour, then transfer to a freezer bag and label.
That way they won't stick together and you can pull out the
required number of meatballs, as and when you need them. The
tomato sauce can also be frozen in freezer bags in single or family
size portions for 1 month or in an airtight container in the fridge.*

Beef Burgers

These are perfect for a summer barbecue, or when your children are demanding a junk food fix. They're tasty, without any unnecessary additives – a guilt-free treat!

PLAN AHEAD
Hob or grill recipe
Double up
and freeze

Serves 6–8

1 onion, finely chopped	1 tsp dried coriander
1 clove garlic, crushed	1 tsp cumin
400g lean beef mince	1 tsp English mustard
1 tbsp home-prepared wholemeal breadcrumbs (page 12)	2 tsp tomato purée
	Seasoning to taste
1 egg, beaten	Olive oil

1   Place the onion and garlic in a large bowl and stir well. Add the mince and breadcrumbs and mix thoroughly.

2   Add the beaten egg (you may not need to use it all), coriander, cumin, mustard and tomato purée. Season to taste.

3   Mix thoroughly and form into balls – these should be firm but moist.

4   Use the palm of your hand to flatten the balls into burger shapes. Place them in the fridge until you are ready to use them, or freeze them in layers (see box opposite).

5   When you are ready to cook, brush the burgers lightly with olive oil. Place under a hot grill or in a frying pan and cook for 5–8 minutes on each side.

6   Garnish with salad and serve in wholemeal baps with **Homemade Potato Wedges** (page 61).

Storage Tip

Freeze some burgers once they are formed, before cooking. Simply shape into patties and pile them one on top of the other, with greaseproof paper between each burger to prevent them from sticking together. Freeze in stacks of 2 or 4, in freezer bags.

Extra Recipes

If you like your burgers slightly spicy, why not add some chopped chillies and 1 teaspoon of curry powder to the burger ingredients before mixing? You could also brush the burgers with chilli oil instead of olive oil to add a tasty zing.

Beef and Bacon Burgers

If I'm making burgers, I like to batch up several variations, such as this one, and pop them into the freezer. I like to use smoked bacon in this recipe as it adds a stronger flavour, but it also works well with unsmoked.

PLAN AHEAD
Hob or grill recipe
**Double up
and freeze**

Serves 4

1 onion, finely chopped

1 clove garlic, crushed

400g beef mince

2–3 rashers of lean bacon, finely chopped

¼ teaspoon marjoram

2 tsp tomato purée

1 tbsp home-prepared wholemeal breadcrumbs (page 12)

1 egg, beaten

2–3 tsp Cajun seasoning

Olive oil for frying

1   Into a large bowl, put the chopped onion and crushed garlic; stir well. Add the mince, bacon, tomato purée and breadcrumbs. Mix thoroughly.

2   Add the beaten egg (you may not need to use it all), marjoram and Cajun seasoning.

3   Combine thoroughly and form into balls – these should be firm but moist. Use the palm of your hand to flatten the balls into burger shapes.

4   Place the burgers in the fridge until needed, or freeze them (see tip on page 133).

5   When you are ready to cook, you can grill the burgers or fry them in a little olive oil for 5–8 minutes on both sides.

7   Serve with wholemeal baps, garnished with salad, and **Homemade Potato Wedges** (page 61).

FISH

We should all try to eat more fish, especially oily fish such as mackerel, pilchards, salmon and tuna as these are rich in omega 3. Get to know your local fishmonger as he/she can offer a wide range of tips, advice and even recipe suggestions, such as the right sauce to accompany your fish. You fishmonger can also clean, fillet and prepare fish ready for cooking, if you don't feel ready to do this yourself.

The recipes in this chapter are all family favourites, ranging from fish pie right through to casseroles and pasta dishes. Some can be prepared in advance and some can be frozen. So, always remember the golden rule: double up the recipe and freeze one dish to always be one step ahead with your very own ready meals.

Italian-style Baked Cod

If you are concerned about using cod, which is often over-fished, you can opt for a more sustainable fish, such as coley or pollock instead. If you are not confident about cooking with fish, speak to your fishmonger as he/she will be able to make great suggestions.

PLAN AHEAD
Slow cooker recipe

Serves 4

12–15 cherry or vine tomatoes	Balsamic vinegar
1 large red onion, sliced	Sprinkling of sugar
Handful of olives, halved or whole, pitted	Sprinkling of sea salt
2–3 garlic cloves	400g cod fillets
Olive oil	Sun-dried tomato pesto
	2–3 sprigs of thyme

1   If your slow cooker needs to be preheated, turn it on 15 minutes before using. Refer to your manufacturer's instructions for more information on your specific model temperatures.

2   Place half the tomatoes, onion, olives and garlic in the base of the slow cooker. Drizzle with olive oil and balsamic vinegar, followed by a sprinkling of sugar and a tiny bit of salt.

3   Spread the top of the cod fillets with a thin layer of pesto and place them on top of the vegetables. Tuck the sprigs of thyme between them.

4   Cover with the remaining vegetables and drizzle with a little more oil and balsamic vinegar.

5   Cook on low for 1½–2 hours, or until the fish is cooked to taste.

6   Serve with a healthy salad and new minted potatoes.

One-pot Roasted Fish, Fennel and Red Onion

The delicate flavour of fennel makes this a sophisticated, but simple supper dish. It's a delicious light meal for a summer evening. Serve with new potatoes and a fresh green salad.

PLAN AHEAD
Oven-cook recipe

Serves 4

300–400g white fish fillets such as dab, coley, cod or pollock

2 lemons (juice one of them)

1 large or 2 small bulbs of fennel, sliced

2 red onions, sliced

2–3 garlic cloves, finely sliced

Olive oil

25g butter

Seasoning to taste

1   Preheat your oven to 190°C (gas mark 5).

2   Clean the fish fillets and season well, then squeeze a little lemon juice over them. Leave to one side.

3   Place the sliced fennel, onion, garlic and one lemon, cut into wedges, in a roasting or baking tray. Drizzle with olive oil and bake in the oven for 15 minutes.

4   Place the fish fillets on top of the vegetables and dot a small knob of butter on each one.

5   Drizzle lemon juice over the dish, season to taste, then cover securely with foil. Bake for another 15–20 minutes until the fish is thoroughly cooked and flakes easily off the fork.

Seafood Aljotta

This is a Maltese fish soup, but as the fish pieces are quite large, I think it makes a really nice main course, especially when served with crusty bread, or even new potatoes and green vegetables. This recipe uses fish pieces, which you can buy as a fish pie mix, normally containing a selection of salmon, haddock, pollock or cod.

PLAN AHEAD
Slow cooker recipe
Double up
and freeze

Serves 4

1 onion, finely chopped

1–2 tbsp sun-dried tomato paste

1 tsp paprika

1 bay leaf

1 tin of chopped tomatoes

250ml white wine

250ml fish stock

100g arborio rice

350g fish pieces

Handful of fresh parsley, finely chopped

1   If your slow cooker needs to be preheated, turn it on 15 minutes before using. Refer to your manufacturer's instructions for more information on your specific model temperatures.

2   Place all the ingredients in the stock pot apart from the fish pieces and the parsley.

3   Cook on high for 1 hour. Add the fish pieces and parsley, then cook on high for another 30 minutes to 1 hour, until the fish is cooked to your taste. Serve immediately.

Fish Burgers

Just like meat or veggie burgers, these can be made in batches and frozen ready for when you want a quick snack (see below). You could experiment by adding some chopped chilli for more of a punch. I have used haddock and white fish fillet in this recipe, but ask your fishmonger for other suggestions.

PLAN AHEAD
Hob recipe
Double up
and freeze

Serves 4

Half a bunch of spring onions, finely chopped	Seasoning to taste
200g haddock fillet, finely chopped	1 egg, beaten
200g white fish fillet, finely chopped	1 tbsp home-prepared wholemeal breadcrumbs (page 12)
1 tsp tarragon	1 tbsp flour
Juice of half a lemon	Olive oil

1 In a large bowl, combine the spring onions, fish fillets, tarragon and lemon juice. Season before adding the beaten egg (you may not need to use all of it), then mix together thoroughly.

2 Gradually incorporate the breadcrumbs and flour until you have a firm but moist mixture. Form into balls, then use the palm of your hand to flatten the balls into burger shapes.

4 You can place the fishburgers in the fridge until you are ready to use them, or freeze them in layers, separating each burger with a sheet of baking parchment to prevent them sticking together.

5 When you are ready to cook the burgers, brush lightly with olive oil. Fry or grill until golden and cooked through.

6 Serve with wholemeal baps and a salad garnish, or **Homemade Potato Wedges** (page 61) and peas for a variation on fish and chips.

Creamy Fish Pie

This is a family favourite and it's a great standby to have in the freezer. Perfect for batch cooking, I tend to make one family portion and several single portions.

PLAN AHEAD
Oven-cook recipe
Double up
and freeze

Serves 4

1kg potatoes	250ml milk
A little butter for mashing	25g butter
500g of fish (this can be fish fillets or chunks, such as haddock, cod, pollock and salmon)	25g flour
	1 tsp mustard
50g prawns, shelled (optional)	Seasoning to taste
	A little grated cheese for topping

1 Preheat your oven to 200°C (gas mark 6).

2 Boil or steam the potatoes until tender. Once cooked, mash with a little butter and place to one side.

3 Meanwhile place the fish, prawns and milk in a pan and bring the milk to the boil. Reduce the heat and cook gently for 10 minutes or until the fish is cooked through.

4 Drain the fish, reserving the liquid to make the sauce. Dice the fish if it is not already cut into chunks and place in a pie dish.

5 To make a creamy sauce, melt the butter in a pan and add the flour. Stir in the reserved milk stock and heat gently until the sauce thickens. I normally use a whisk at this stage as it helps to prevent any lumps from forming. Stir continuously.

6 Add the mustard and season to taste once the sauce is the right consistency, then pour it over the fish.

7   Cover the fish with the mashed potato and top with a small
    amount of grated cheese. You can freeze the dish at this point (once
    cooled) or continue to bake in the oven for 20–25 minutes, until
    golden and bubbling.

Top Tip

*Your fishmonger will often sell fish pie mix (a selection of fish) or
he/she may have some odd bits they can pop together for you at
a discounted price.*

Extra Recipes

*Add sweet potato and carrot to the mash for the top of this pie.
You can even add a few handfuls of crushed peas – they taste
divine and go really well with the fish.*

Salmon, Sweet Potato and Chilli Fish Cakes

These fish cakes are a tasty way to get your Omega 3. They also freeze well, so why not make more than you need and batch them up for the freezer to eat another day?

PLAN AHEAD
Hob or grill recipe
Double up
and freeze

Serves 4

50g breadcrumbs (page 12)

2 tbsp semolina

Seasoning

300g fresh or tinned salmon

350g sweet potatoes, cooked and mashed

3 spring onions, finely chopped

2 chillies, deseeded and finely chopped

1 tsp ground cumin

1 tbsp lemon juice

Small handful of fresh coriander leaves, finely chopped

2 eggs, beaten

Plain flour (optional)

1   Combine the breadcrumbs and the semolina, season and leave to one side.

2   Mix the salmon, sweet potato, spring onions, chillies, cumin, lemon juice and coriander together in a bowl. Add a little beaten egg to bind, if needed. Season to taste.

3   Form the mixture into fish cakes; if it is too wet, add a little plain flour.

4   To coat the fish cakes, brush with a little beaten egg, then dip into the breadcrumb mixture. This is messy, so be prepared! Place the fish cakes on greased baking parchment and chill in the fridge for 10 minutes to help them firm up. You can now continue to cook them, or freeze them on the tray, layer up with a sheet of baking parchment between each cake and transfer them to a freezer bag.

5   To cook the cakes, grill or fry them until golden. Serve with a green salad and new potatoes.

Haddock, Egg and Gruyère Bake

This is such a quick and easy dish, and perfect for a comforting supper. Get ahead of yourself and prepare it before you go to work, then when you get home you can have dinner on the table in just 20 minutes.

PLAN AHEAD
Oven-cook recipe
Double up
and freeze

Serves 4

400g haddock fillets, roughly chopped

2–3 hard-boiled eggs, halved or quartered

200ml crème fraîche

150ml milk

125g Gruyère cheese, grated

2 tsp wholegrain mustard

Seasoning

2 tbsp breadcrumbs (page 12)

1 tbsp oats

50g Parmesan cheese, grated

1   Preheat your oven to 180°C (gas mark 4).

2   Place the haddock and hard-boiled eggs in an ovenproof dish.

3   In a bowl, combine the crème fraîche, milk, grated Gruyère cheese and mustard. Season to taste. Spoon this over the egg and haddock mixture.

4   Mix the breadcrumbs, oats and Parmesan together, season well and sprinkle over the crème fraîche mixture. Freeze at this point.

5   Place in the oven and bake for 15–20 minutes, until the haddock is cooked.

Tomato and Tuna Gratin

Another great store-cupboard meal for when you are in a hurry. This recipe can be prepared ahead and just popped into the oven to bake when you get home.

PLAN AHEAD
Oven-cook recipe

Serves 4

400g tinned tuna

Olive oil

1 red onion, finely chopped

2 garlic cloves, crushed

Half a red pepper, deseeded and diced

400g tin of chopped tomatoes

Dash of balsamic vinegar

Small handful of fresh basil, chopped

½ tsp dried thyme

Seasoning to taste

75g breadcrumbs (page 12)

50g oats

50g mature Cheddar, grated

1   Preheat your oven to 200°C (gas mark 6).

2   Break the tuna into chunks with a fork, and place in the bottom of an ovenproof dish.

3   Heat the olive oil in a sauté pan. Add the onion, garlic and red pepper and cook until it starts to soften. Add the chopped tomatoes, balsamic vinegar and herbs. Season to taste, then pour over the tuna.

4   In a bowl, mix the breadcrumbs, oats and grated cheese. Season to taste and sprinkle over the tomato mixture.

5   Place in the oven on a low rack and cook for 15 minutes.

Baked Herbie Salmon

This is a really simple recipe that looks quite impressive when served. You can parcel up the fish and refrigerate until you are ready to cook.

PLAN AHEAD
Oven-cook recipe

Serves 4

Handful of fresh basil leaves	Butter for greasing
Small handful of fresh dill	1 red onion, sliced
Juice of two lemons	400g large salmon fillets (enough
30–40ml olive oil	to serve 4), boned, trimmed
	and ready to cook

1 Preheat the oven to 200°C (gas mark 6).

2 Place the herbs, lemon juice and olive oil in a food processor and whizz until combined.

3 Butter a sheet of tin foil large enough to wrap around the salmon and add the sliced onion. Place one of the salmon fillets over the onion.

4 Spread the herby paste over the salmon, then place the remaining fillet on top.

5 Wrap the salmon in the foil, making sure the edges are sealed well, and lay it on a baking tray.

6 Place the salmon in the oven and bake for 20–25 minutes depending on the size of the fish, until the fish flakes easily.

7 Unwrap the foil parcel, slice the fish and serve with new potatoes and green vegetables.

Creamy Baked Haddock

This is one of those suppers that is really comforting, especially on a cold winter evening. It can be prepared in advance and kept in the refrigerator until it's time to cook.

PLAN AHEAD
Oven-cook recipe

Serves 4

40g butter, plus extra for greasing

800g haddock fillets (unsmoked)

Seasoning to taste

1 red onion, sliced

Juice and zest of one lemon

2 tsp wholegrain mustard

150ml crème fraîche

150ml milk

Small handful of freshly chopped parsley

Black pepper

Parmesan cheese, grated

1 Preheat the oven to 190°C (gas mark 5).

2 Butter the base of an ovenproof dish.

3 Spread or dot butter over the haddock fillets and season before roughly chopping them. Place these in the ovenproof dish with the sliced onion.

4 In a bowl, mix the lemon zest and juice, mustard, crème fraîche, milk and parsley. Season with black pepper and combine well.

5 Pour the creamy sauce over the fish and spread evenly. Sprinkle with grated Parmesan and black pepper. Place in the oven and bake for 20–25 minutes until the fish is tender.

Salmon with a Honey and Mustard Crust

A simple yet delicious dish that makes the most of this healthy, oily fish. The salmon can be prepared in advance and kept in the refrigerator until needed.

PLAN AHEAD
Oven-cook recipe

Serves 4

Juice of half a lemon
400g salmon fillets
1–2 tbsp wholegrain mustard
1–2 tbsp honey

2–3 tbsp wholemeal breadcrumbs (page 12)
2–3 tbsp cornflakes, crushed (if you don't have cornflakes, use finely chopped nuts)

1 Preheat the oven to 200°C (gas mark 6).
2 Drizzle the lemon juice over your salmon fillets.
3 Mix the mustard and honey together in a bowl. In another bowl, combine the breadcrumbs and cornflakes.
4 Spread the mustard coating over the salmon, ensuring the tops are well coated. Dip these into the breadcrumb mixture, again ensuring they are well coated.
5 Arrange the fillets on a baking tray and bake in the oven for 12–15 minutes, until the fillets are cooked.
6 Serve with a green salad and new potatoes.

Tomato, Prawn and Fish Stew

An easy, one-pot recipe that you can cook on the hob. It's ready in 30 minutes and needs no more than a hunk of crusty bread to go with it.

PLAN AHEAD
Hob recipe

Serves 4

1–2 tbsp olive oil	300ml white wine
1 onion, finely chopped	350g fish fillets or pieces
2 garlic cloves, crushed	12 prawns (shelled)
1 red pepper, deseeded and diced	Seasoning to taste
1 tin of chopped tomatoes, or 6 skinned ripe tomatoes	2 bay leaves
300ml warm fish stock	A handful of fresh parsley, chopped

1   Heat the oil in a casserole pan and fry the onion, garlic and pepper for 2–3 minutes.

2   Add all the remaining ingredients except for the parsley and combine well. Season to taste.

3   Cover with a lid and cook on a very gentle simmer for 30 minutes.

4   Serve in bowls with a sprinkling of chopped parsley.

Cod and Cheese Gratin

Some people scorn fish and cheese combinations, but personally I find them quite comforting. After I've had a hard day, I find this particular dish helps to make things seem a little bit better.

PLAN AHEAD

Oven-cook recipe
Double up
and freeze

Serves 4

250g crème fraîche	Seasoning to taste
Small handful of fresh parsley, chopped	300–400g skinless cod fillets, roughly chopped
1 tsp wholegrain mustard	100g oats
100g mature Cheddar cheese, grated	100g breadcrumbs (page 12)
	50g Parmesan cheese, grated

1   Preheat the oven to 180°C (gas mark 4).

2   Mix the crème fraîche, parsley, mustard and cheese in a bowl. Season to taste.

3   Place the fish pieces in an ovenproof dish and pour over the crème fraîche mixture.

4   Mix the oats, breadcrumbs and Parmesan together. Season and sprinkle on top of the crème fraîche mixture. Freeze at this point.

5   Place in the oven and bake for 15–20 minutes.

Salmon and Herb Butter Parcels

This recipe uses herb butter. Use some you have prepared earlier and have stashed in your freezer (page 12) or double up the herb butter in this recipe to make extra for your freezer.

PLAN AHEAD
Oven-cook recipe

Serves 4

1–2 tbsp butter, softened

Small handful of fresh herbs, such as dill and parsley, finely chopped

400g salmon fillets

1 lemon, sliced

Olive oil

Black pepper

1   Preheat the oven to 200°C (gas mark 6).

2   Mix the butter and herbs together in a bowl to form a herb butter.

3   Cut four squares of tin foil, larger than each salmon fillet.

4   Dot each fillet with herb butter, a slice or two of lemon and 1 dessertspoon of water. Drizzle with olive oil and season with black pepper.

5   Seal the foil parcels and place them on a baking tray or directly on the low rack. Bake for 15–20 minutes until the fish is tender and flaking.

6   Serve with new potatoes and green vegetables.

Haddock Florentine

Haddock is not overly fishy, so it's a good choice for the more fussy eaters in your family. This is another great, supper meal.

PLAN AHEAD
Oven-cook recipe

Serves 4

180g spinach	100g mature Cheddar
500–700ml milk	1 tsp wholegrain mustard
400g haddock fillets	Pinch of cayenne pepper
20g butter	Seasoning to taste
20g plain flour	

1   Preheat the oven to 200°C (gas mark 6).

2   Steam the spinach for 5 minutes to wilt it. Once soft, place in a greased ovenproof dish and press down to form a base.

3   Bring the milk to the boil and add the haddock fillets. Reduce the heat and simmer gently until the haddock is cooked and flaking off the fork. Remove the fish from the milk (reserve the milk) and flake it onto the bed of spinach.

4   Meanwhile, melt the butter in a saucepan. Add the flour to form a paste. Gradually add the hot milk that you cooked the haddock in and stir well. Use a balloon whisk to remove any lumps.

5   Add almost all the cheese, retaining some for the topping, then stir in the mustard and cayenne pepper and season to taste. Once the cheese is melted, pour the sauce over the haddock mixture.

6   Garnish with the remaining cheese and place in the oven to bake for 10–15 minutes, until golden on top.

Smoked Mackerel and Leek Pie

I have added sweet potato to the pie mash as it not only adds a fantastic colour, but is packed with antioxidants.

PLAN AHEAD
Oven-cook recipe
Double up
and freeze

Serves 4

500g potatoes	150ml cream cheese
250g sweet potato	150ml milk
Knob of butter	50g Parmesan cheese, grated
2 leeks, diced	Small handful of freshly chopped parsley
400g smoked mackerel fillets, diced	Seasoning to taste
300ml crème fraîche	

1 Preheat the oven to 200°C (gas mark 6).

2 Cut the potatoes and sweet potatoes into equal-sized chunks, then place them in a pan to steam.

3 Fry the leeks in a little butter to help soften them.

4 Place the softened leeks in a bowl and add the mackerel, crème fraîche, cream cheese, milk, Parmesan and parsley. Mix thoroughly and season to taste. If the mixture looks too dry, add a little more milk.

5 Transfer the mixture to a 2.5 litre ovenproof dish.

6 Mash the potatoes with a little butter, season well and then use to top the mackerel mixture.

7 Place the pie in the oven and bake for 20 minutes until golden.

Cheesy Pollock Layer

If you don't want to use pollock you can opt for cod or even coley.

PLAN AHEAD
Oven-cook recipe

Serves 4

Juice and zest of one lemon

400g pollock fillets

100g baby leaf spinach

3 tomatoes, sliced

Seasoning to taste

250g crème fraîche

200ml milk

100g Parmesan cheese, grated

40g breadcrumbs (page 12)

40g oats

1 Preheat the oven to 200°C (gas mark 6).

2 Drizzle the lemon juice over the fish fillets and leave to one side.

3 In the base of an ovenproof dish, place a layer of spinach leaves. On top of this, add the slices of tomato. Season with black pepper.

4 Place the fish fillets over the tomatoes. Add any remaining lemon juice and the lemon zest.

5 In a bowl, combine the crème fraîche, milk and 75g of the grated Parmesan cheese. Season to taste before pouring this over the fish fillets.

6 In another bowl, mix the breadcrumbs, oats and remaining Parmesan. Mix and season well, then sprinkle this over the sauce.

7 Place in the oven and bake for 25 minutes, until golden.

Top Tip

Both Smoked Mackerel and Leek Pie and Cheesy Pollock Layer can be frozen before baking. May be cooked from frozen (or allow to defrost thoroughly). If cooking from frozen, add 10 minutes to the cooking time.

Thai Fish Bakes

You can use whatever fish you prefer in this recipe. Simply pre-pare the Thai sauce, pour over the fish and secure in foil. For added flavour, the fish is marinated in the sauce for an hour be-fore baking, but you can omit this step if you are short of time.

PLAN AHEAD
Oven-cook recipe
Double up
and freeze

Serves 4

3cm piece of fresh ginger

2–3 chillies, deseeded

1–2 stalks of lemon grass

Juice and zest of 1 lime

3–4 lime leaves

4 tsp of Thai paste (red or green)

400g tin of coconut milk

150ml Greek yoghurt

Small handful of fresh Coriander leaves, chopped

Seasoning

350g fish fillets

400g cooked Thai Lime Rice (I use the rice sachets you can buy in supermarkets, or use basmati if you cannot get Thai Lime Rice)

1   Prepare the sauce by blending the ginger, chillies, lemon grass, lime juice and zest, lime leaves, Thai paste, coconut milk and Greek yoghurt and half the coriander leaves together in a food processor. Season to taste.

2   Place the fish fillets each on their own double-layer tinfoil square, large enough to fold and secure into parcels.

3   Pour over the Thai sauce, dividing evenly between each portion. If there is any sauce left, leave it to one side for later.

4   Leave the fish to marinate for at least 1 hour.

5   Preheat the oven to 180°C (gas mark 4). Place the parcels in the oven and cook for 15 minutes.

6   Meanwhile, cook the rice or, if you are using pre-cooked, ready-prepared Thai rice, undo each parcel after the cooking time. Add a portion of rice to each parcel of fish, share out any remaining sauce and reseal the foil parcels. Place back in the oven and cook for a further 5–8 minutes.

8   To serve, garnish with the remaining coriander leaves.

— **Top Tip** —

You could use a Thai meal kit for this recipe, which contains coconut milk, Thai paste, herbs and spices – you may even find this is cheaper than buying each item individually.

Salmon, Ricotta and Cheese Cannelloni

Use tinned salmon if you prefer, as you need to cook and flake the salmon for this recipe.

PLAN AHEAD
Oven-cook recipe
Double up
and freeze

Serves 4

50g fresh baby leaf spinach

300g salmon fillets, cooked and shredded

250g tub of ricotta

Zest of one lemon, finely chopped

Small handful of fresh dill, finely chopped

Generous pinch of grated nutmeg

8 dried lasagne sheets

500g crème fraîche

1 small red onion, finely chopped

75g mature Cheddar, grated

Seasoning

50g breadcrumbs (page 12)

30g Parmesan cheese, grated

1   Place the spinach in a colander and rinse it under hot water for a couple of seconds to wilt the leaves.

2   In a bowl, mix together the salmon, ricotta, baby leaf spinach, lemon zest, dill and grated nutmeg.

3   Cook the lasagne sheets in boiling water for 5–8 minutes. Drain and lay them flat, then divide the salmon and ricotta mixture between them, laying it in a line at one end of each sheet. Roll up firmly to form tubes, then place them, with the seal on the base, in a single layer in an ovenproof dish.

4   Preheat the oven to 190°C (gas mark 5).

5   Mix the crème fraîche, onion, cheese and seasoning together. Pour this over the cannelloni. Sprinkle with a mixture of the breadcrumbs and Parmesan before baking in the oven for 35–40 minutes.

6   Serve with garlic bread and a green salad.

Salmon, Garlic and White Wine Parcels

This recipe takes only minutes to prepare and parcel up, making it a great dinner party meal. Just pop them in the oven when you are ready to cook.

PLAN AHEAD
Oven-cook recipe

Serves 4

3–4 garlic cloves, crushed	Butter for greasing
1 tbsp honey	1 small onion, sliced into rings
1 tbsp wholegrain mustard	4 salmon fillets
1 tbsp balsamic vinegar	Small handful of fresh dill, finely chopped
2 tbsp white wine	
Zest of one lemon	Seasoning to taste

1   Preheat the oven to 200°C (gas mark 6) if you are cooking the parcels straight away.

2   Place the garlic, honey, mustard, balsamic vinegar, white wine and lemon zest in a bowl and combine well.

3   Prepare four foil squares, double thickness and big enough to parcel the salmon fillets individually. Butter the foil and add the sliced onion, then lay salmon fillet on each piece of foil.

4   Spoon the garlic sauce over the salmon fillets, ensuring they are coated. Add a sprinkling of dill and season to taste.

5   Parcel up the salmon fillets, making sure the edges are well sealed. These can be left in the fridge until needed.

6   When you are ready to cook, arrange the salmon parcels on a baking tray. Place in the oven and cook for 15–20 minutes until the fish flakes easily.

7   Unwrap and serve with new potatoes and green vegetables.

Salmon and Prawn Puff Pie

You can prepare this in advance and bake it the next day, or even freeze, unbaked, until needed another time. Allow the pie to defrost completely before baking.

PLAN AHEAD
Oven-cook recipe
Double up
and freeze

Serves 4–6

300g crème fraîche	Flour for rolling out
250ml milk	150g prawns (shelled)
1 tsp wholegrain mustard	50g baby leaf spinach, shredded
Seasoning to taste	125g ready-made puff pastry
50g watercress, finely chopped	Milk for brushing
500g salmon fillet pieces	2 tsp sesame seeds

1 Preheat the oven to 200°C (gas mark 6) if you are cooking this straight away.

2 In a bowl, combine the crème fraîche, milk and mustard. Season to taste before adding the chopped watercress.

3 Place the salmon, prawns and spinach in an ovenproof dish and make sure that they are well combined. Pour over the crème fraîche mixture and combine again.

4 On a floured surface, roll the pastry out to 2–3mm thickness and use it to cover the pie. Brush with a little milk and sprinkle with the sesame seeds. You can freeze at this point.

5 When you are ready to cook, place the pie in the oven and bake for 25 minutes until the puff pastry top has risen and is golden. Serve immediately.

Smoked Haddock with Leek and Parsley Sauce

A lovely supper meal – you can use smoked or unsmoked haddock to suit your own taste, or a mixture of the two, if you prefer.

PLAN AHEAD
Hob recipe

Serves 4

25g butter plus extra for frying	Seasoning to taste
1 tbsp plain flour or cornflour	4 leeks, cleaned and sliced
500ml milk	400g smoked haddock fillets
Handful of fresh parsley, finely chopped	

1   To make the sauce, place the butter in a saucepan and gently melt over medium heat. Add the flour or cornflour and stir well with a wooden spoon to form a paste. Add a little milk at a time, continuing to stir to avoid lumps.

2   Switch to using a balloon whisk: continue to stir over a medium heat until the sauce begins to thicken. The balloon whisk will also help eradicate any lumps that may have materialised. Add more milk as necessary to achieve the desired thickness, i.e. the consistency of custard.

3   Add the parsley to the sauce and season with black pepper.

4   In a large pan, add a knob of butter and the leeks. Fry for 2–3 minutes, then cover with a lid and sweat for 5–10 minutes until softened. Add them to the parsley sauce.

5   Five minutes before serving, cook the fish by placing the haddock fillets in a large pan of simmering water and poach for 5 minutes, until the flesh flakes easily.

6   Place the fillets on serving plates, then cover with a spoonful of the leek and parsley sauce. Serve with new potatoes and green beans.

Halibut, Chilli and Vegetable Casserole

This dish is also good with cod or haddock. Fish does not require a long cooking time, so when using a slow cooker, add the fish at a late stage.

PLAN AHEAD

Slow cooker recipe
Double up
and freeze

Serves 4

1 red onion, sliced	400g tin of chopped tomatoes
1–2 peppers, deseeded and sliced	2 tsp sun-dried tomato paste
1–2 chillies, deseeded and finely sliced (to taste)	½ tsp chilli powder
	1 tsp paprika
2 sweet potatoes, diced	200ml white wine
2 small potatoes, diced	200ml fish stock
1–2 carrots, diced	2 courgettes, thickly sliced
2 sticks of celery, diced	500g halibut fillets, diced

1   If your slow cooker needs to be preheated, turn it on 15 minutes before using. Refer to the manufacturer's instructions for more information on your specific model temperatures.

2   Prepare the vegetables and chillies, making sure they are cut to equal size and thickness. This dish works best if you leave the vegetables chunky.

3   Add everything apart from the courgettes and halibut to the slow cooker. Make sure the fish stock is hot when you add it.

4   Cook for 6–8 hours on low. An hour before serving, switch to high and add the courgettes and halibut. Test the fish before serving to make sure that it is tender and cooked. Cool thoroughly before freezing.

5   Serve with rice, cous cous or quinoa.

Prawn and Asparagus Pasta

A really simple recipe that can be made in the time it takes to boil your pasta! Asparagus is available all year round from the supermarket, but in the UK the best time to buy is during the season, which can be any time from the end of April to mid-June.

PLAN AHEAD
Hob recipe

Serves 4

300g penne pasta

200g asparagus spears

75g frozen peas

1 tbsp olive oil

1–2 garlic cloves, crushed

200g prawns (shelled)

200g low-fat crème fraîche

Zest and juice of half a lemon

Black pepper

1   Place the pasta in boiling, salted water and cook as directed on the packet. Four to five minutes before the pasta is ready, add the asparagus spears and frozen peas to the pan.

2   Meanwhile, heat the olive oil in a pan and add the garlic. Cook for 1 minute, then add the prawns and cook until they are transparent. Add the crème fraîche, lemon zest and juice. Season with black pepper.

3   Drain the pasta and return it to the saucepan. Add the prawn sauce and stir well over low heat to combine, then serve immediately.

VEGETARIAN

You don't have to be a vegetarian to enjoy veggie meals. There is a wide variety of meals in this chapter, and some, like the Lentil Dahl (opposite), can be used as a side dish, others for a main meal. It is good for your health to have meat-free days, so choose from these delicious recipes to broaden your family repertoire.

The recipes in this section are family favourites ranging from Vegetable Mornay Bake (page 174) right through to nut roasts, casseroles and pasta dishes. Some can be prepared in advance; some can be frozen. So, remember the golden rule as you plan your cooking: double up the recipe and freeze one to always be one step ahead and create your very own ready meals.

Lentil Dahl

This is so easy to make and costs very little.

PLAN AHEAD

Hob recipe
Double up
and freeze

Serves 4

1 tsp olive oil or coconut oil

1 onion, chopped

2 garlic cloves, crushed

1 pepper, deseeded and chopped (optional)

100g red lentils

3–5cm piece of fresh ginger

3 heaped tsp mild or sweet curry powder

1–2 tsp turmeric

3 tomatoes, finely chopped

1 tsp tomato purée

300–400ml hot water (start by using only the 300ml)

2 tbsp low-fat crème fraîche or 0-per cent fat Greek yoghurt (optional)

1   Place the olive oil or coconut oil in a heavy based pan over a medium heat. Add the chopped onion, garlic and pepper and cook for 5 minutes until they start to soften.

2   Add the remaining ingredients and allow to simmer gently on the hob, stirring occasionally to avoid the dahl sticking to the base. Don't have the heat too high: it's better to cook slowly on a lower heat.

4   As the lentils start to break down, the mixture will thicken to a rich golden dahl. Add more liquid if it looks too thick or dry.

5   If you like a creamier dahl, stir in a couple of tablespoons of crème fraîche or Greek yoghurt right at the end of the cooking time.

Healthy Tip

Lentils can help to lower cholesterol and balance blood sugars and are an excellent source of protein, fibre, B vitamins and minerals.

Vegetable Korma

Forget the calorie-laden kormas – this is a great, healthy recipe for vegetarians and meat eaters alike. I like to make a selection of curries and serve them together so you can mix up the flavours.

PLAN AHEAD
Slow cook recipe
Double up
and freeze

Serves 4

2 tbsp olive oil

2 garlic cloves

2–3cm piece of fresh ginger

1–2 tbsp korma curry powder

1 tbsp garam masala

½ tsp cumin

½ tsp turmeric

¼ tsp nutmeg

1 tbsp ground almonds

2–3 tomatoes

1 large onion, diced

1 pepper, deseeded and diced

2 sweet potatoes, diced

2 potatoes, diced

1 large carrot, diced

½ head of cauliflower

400g tin of chickpeas, drained

300–450ml vegetable stock or water

2–3 handfuls of baby leaf spinach

2 courgettes, thickly sliced

4–5 tbsp thick 0-per cent fat Greek yoghurt

1   In a food processor, blitz the oil, garlic, ginger, spices, almonds and tomatoes to form a paste.

2   Chop the vegetables so they are roughly all the same size.

3   If your slow cooker needs to be preheated, turn it on 15 minutes before using. Refer to your manufacturer's instructions for more information on your specific model temperatures.

4   Place the vegetables (but not the spinach or courgettes) and chickpeas in the slow cooker. Pour on the curry paste and 300ml vegetable stock or water and combine well. Add more stock if you need to but remember the stock does not evaporate, so if you want a thicker

sauce, don't add too much. If, during cooking, you think you have
added too much water, mix some cornflour with water to form a
paste and stir this into the korma; alternatively, throw in a large
handful of red lentils.

5 Cook on low for 6–8 hours. One hour before serving, mix in the
spinach, courgettes and Greek yoghurt. Turn to high and continue
to cook for the remaining hour.

6 Serve with rice and Indian chutneys.

Storage Tip

*If you love curries, double up the recipes in this book whenever
you make one and freeze smaller portions ready to make a
lovely selection and invite friends for a curry night. They will
be impressed by your hard work, but all you have to do on the
night is reheat and enjoy the evening.*

Mushroom Risotto

Risottos are very easy as long as you take things nice and slowly and not try to rush each stage.

PLAN AHEAD
Hob recipe

Serves 4

2 tsp dried porcini mushrooms

Olive oil

Knob of butter

1 onion, finely chopped

400g mixed fresh mushrooms (shiitake, oyster, chestnut, wild, etc)

500–700ml vegetable stock (or the water from soaking the mushrooms)

300g risotto rice

200ml white wine

Handful of fresh tarragon, chopped

Zest of half a lemon

2–3 tbsp low-fat crème fraîche (optional)

Handful of fresh, chopped herbs like parsley and tarragon

Parmesan cheese, to serve

1   Soak the porcini mushrooms as directed on the packet. This normally takes 20 minutes. Retain the fluid to add to your stock.

2   Place a splash of olive oil and a knob of butter in the base of a saucepan. Add the chopped onion and fry until translucent. Add the fresh and dried mushrooms, and stir well.

3   Add the rice and stir in, ensuring that the rice is completely covered in the oil and butter mixture. Don't let this stick – if necessary, keep the heat to a medium rather than full.

4   Add the wine and stir thoroughly. The wine will evaporate but will flavour the rice.

5   Add the stock (ideally warm or hot stock), a ladleful at a time. Wait until the stock has been soaked up by the rice before adding more.

6   After 10–15 minutes the rice should be tender (not soft as it should still have a little bite to it). After adding the final stock, add tarragon and lemon zest. For a creamy risotto, stir in the crème fraîche.

7   Serve immediately, garnished with chopped herbs and Parmesan.

Ratatouille

A batch of this in the freezer can be used as a base for a vegetable lasagne, a topping for a pizza or even be mixed with pasta.

PLAN AHEAD
Hob recipe
Double up
and freeze

Serves 4

2 tbsp olive oil	400g tin chopped tomatoes
1 aubergine, diced	2 tsp tomato purée
2 courgettes, sliced	100ml red wine
1 red onion, sliced	Handful of chopped fresh herbs
1–2 garlic cloves, crushed	(I use oregano, thyme and parsley)
1–2 red peppers, deseeded and sliced	Black pepper

1   In a large sauté pan, fry the aubergine and courgettes in olive oil for 5 minutes until slightly charred. Remove and place on a plate until later. (I usually place a piece of kitchen towel over the plate to soak up any excess oil).

2   Add the onion, garlic and peppers and cook for 3–4 minutes, then add the tomatoes, tomato purée and the wine.

3   Return the aubergines and courgettes to the pan, then add the fresh herbs and seasoning. Cover with a lid, reduce the heat to low and cook slowly for 10 minutes, until the mixture reduces slightly.

4   Serve or allow to cool, ready to freeze.

Tuscan Tomato and Beans

One of my favourite lunches, like a posh, home-made serving of baked beans. Packed with protein and fibre, it makes a great, slow-release energy meal, but cooks in just 20 minutes.

PLAN AHEAD
Hob recipe

Serves 4

1 large red onion, chopped

2–3 garlic cloves, roughly chopped

1 red pepper, deseeded diced

1 stick of celery, diced

1–2 tbsp olive oil

1kg fresh tomatoes, chopped and skinned

200ml red wine or vegetable stock

2 tins of borlotti or cannellini beans, drained (or one of each)

½ tsp dried thyme

½ tsp dried oregano

1 tsp dried parsley

1 tsp sugar

Sprinkling of salt and pepper

1 tsp balsamic vinegar (optional)

Fresh parsley, chopped (for garnish)

100g feta cheese, crumbled

1 Place the onion, garlic, pepper and celery in a heavy based pan with a little olive oil on a medium heat.

2 Cook for 5 minutes until they start to soften, then add all the other ingredients apart from the feta cheese; combine well. Cook for 10 minutes on a medium heat.

3 Serve with a sprinkling of fresh parsley, crumbled feta cheese and warm crusty bread.

Tofu and Chickpea Burgers

I love these burgers. If you like them to taste very spicy, double up the chillies and add a splash of Tabasco sauce.

PLAN AHEAD
Hob or grill recipe
Double up
and freeze

Serves 4–6

400g tin chickpeas, drained	1 tsp tomato purée
250g firm tofu	1–2 tsp garam masala
1 onion, finely chopped	Splash of soy sauce
1–2 garlic cloves, crushed	Seasoning to taste
1 chilli, finely chopped	1 tbsp home-prepared wholemeal
1 celery stick, finely chopped	breadcrumbs (page 12)
	1 tbsp oats

1 Put the chickpeas in a large bowl and mash until soft. Add the tofu and continue to mash until the two are thoroughly mixed together.

2 Deseed and finely chop the chilli. Fry with the onion, garlic, and celery until softened. Add to the chickpea and tofu mixture.

3 Add the tomato purée, garam masala, soy sauce and seasoning. Stir well before adding the breadcrumbs and oats.

4 Mix thoroughly and form into firm but moist balls (on a floured surface if the mixture is sticky). Use the palm of your hand to flatten the balls into burger shapes.

5 You can place the burgers in the fridge until you are ready to use them, or freeze them in layers (separate each layer with baking parchment to prevent them sticking together).

6 When you are ready to cook the burgers, brush lightly with olive oil. Grill or fry for 5–8 minutes on each side until golden.

7 Serve in wholemeal baps, garnished with salad, and **Homemade Potato Wedges** (p61).

Thai Bean Cakes

This is a versatile recipe that can be adapted to suit what is in your store cupboard. If you don't have cannellini beans, use chickpeas or butterbeans. This also works well with left-over mashed potato – a sort of Thai potato cake!

PLAN AHEAD
Hob recipe
Double up
and freeze

Serves 4

1 tin of cannellini beans

Half a bunch of spring onions, finely chopped

Handful of fresh coriander leaves, finely chopped

2–3 tsp red Thai paste

Zest of one lime

Juice of half a lime

Flour for dusting

1–2 tbsp olive oil

Sweet chilli sauce, to serve

1   Drain the beans into a colander and rinse in cold water. Shake dry.

2   Place the beans, spring onions, coriander, Thai paste and zest and juice of lime in a food processor. Whizz until combined.

3   Tip the mixture onto a floured board and shape into 4–6 patties with your hands.

4   Heat the olive oil in sauté pan and fry the bean cakes on both sides until golden. Serve with the sweet chilli sauce

Mushroom and Goats' Cheese Bakes

Serve this with a roast as an alternative to meat or with a salad on a summer's day. The combination of red onion, mushroom and goats' cheese is divine!

PLAN AHEAD
Hob and grill recipe

Serves 4

4–6 large portobello mushrooms

30g butter, melted

Olive oil

1 red onion, sliced

2 gloves of garlic, crushed

1 dessertspoon of balsamic vinegar

1 dessertspoon of brown sugar

100g goats' cheese, crumbled

Black pepper

1   Brush the mushrooms with a little melted butter and place under a hot grill for 8–10 minutes.

2   While the mushrooms are grilling, place a little olive oil in a sauté pan over a medium heat. Add the onions and garlic and cook until softened.

3   Add the balsamic vinegar and sugar and cook for another 5 minutes to caramelise the onions.

4   Remove the mushrooms from the grill. Add a little of the onion mix to each mushroom and finish with a crumbling of goats' cheese. Season with black pepper.

5   Place the mushrooms back under the grill and cook for another few minutes until the goats' cheese is golden.

Extra Recipes

Instead of goats' cheese, try crumbling Stilton or another blue cheese over the mushrooms.

Leek and Cheese Sausages

Another great meat-free alternative! Serve as a vegetarian option alongside meaty sausages, or cook them on the barbecue.

PLAN AHEAD

Hob or grill recipe
Oven-cook recipe
**Double up
and freeze**

Serves 4

For the sausages

125g wholemeal breadcrumbs
(page 12)

30g oats

150g mature Cheddar cheese,
grated

1 egg, beaten

30–40ml milk

1 leek, finely chopped

1 tsp wholegrain mustard

1 tsp thyme

Seasoning to taste

For the coating

1 egg, beaten

30g semolina

30g fine oatmeal

20g plain flour

30g Parmesan cheese, finely
grated

Seasoning to taste

1   Place the breadcrumbs, oats, cheese, egg, milk, leek, mustard and thyme in a bowl and mix well. Season to taste. If too wet, add more breadcrumbs; if too dry, add a little milk. The dough should be firm enough to form thick sausages.

2   Take two shallow bowls. Add the beaten egg to one bowl and in a second bowl, mix the semolina, oatmeal, flour and Parmesan. Season to taste.

3   Dip each sausage into the egg mixture followed by the flour mixture, before placing on a floured sheet of baking parchment.

4   Place in the fridge to rest for at least 30 minutes. You can freeze the
    sausages at this stage.

5   When you are ready to cook the sausages, you can do this under the
    grill, turning regularly until golden, fry in some olive or coconut oil,
    or bake in the oven for 15–20 minutes until golden.

Storage Tip

*Place the sausages on a baking tray covered in baking
parchment. Put the tray straight into the freezer if possible so
they freeze without sticking together. Once frozen, you can then
place them in a freezer bag for storage.*

Vegetable Mornay Bake

I was a vegetarian for many years and this was one of my favourite dishes. I used to serve it with new or roasted potatoes and green vegetables but you can also use this as a side dish for a roast dinner.

PLAN AHEAD

Oven-cook recipe
Double up
and freeze

Serves 4–6

2 carrots

2 leeks

1 small head of broccoli

1 small cauliflower

25g butter

1 tbsp plain flour or cornflour

500–750ml milk

2 tbsp nutritional yeast flakes
(optional)

100g mature Cheddar cheese,
grated (75g for the sauce, 25g
for the topping)

½ tsp mustard

Black pepper to taste

2 tbsp oats

2–3 tbsp home-prepared wholemeal breadcrumbs (page 12)

25g Parmesan cheese

1 Chop the carrots into batons, slice the leeks and cut the broccoli and cauliflower into manageable florets.

2 Place the vegetables in a steamer and cook until the cauliflower is tender but not soft.

3 Meanwhile, make the sauce. Gently melt the butter in a saucepan on medium heat. Add the flour or cornflour and stir well with a wooden spoon. Add the milk a little at a time, continuing to stir to avoid lumps.

4 Switch to using a balloon whisk. Continue to stir over a medium heat until the sauce begins to thicken. The balloon whisk will also

help to eradicate any lumps that may have formed. Add more milk as necessary to achieve the desired thickness. The sauce should be the consistency of custard.

5 If you are using nutritional yeast flakes, add these before the grated cheese as they will reduce the amount of cheese you will need – taste as you go. Add the cheese and mustard and stir well, then season with black pepper.

6 When the vegetables are tender, transfer them to an ovenproof dish. Pour over the sauce ensuring all the vegetables are covered.

7 Mix the oats, breadcrumbs and Parmesan together thoroughly and scatter the mixture over the cheese sauce.

8 You can now leave the dish to cool and freeze, leave it in the fridge until you are ready to cook or bake it immediately in a preheated oven at 180°C (gas mark 4).

9 Cook for 15–20 minutes until golden and bubbling.

Spicy Bean and Tomato
Stuffed Butternut Squash

If you have not tried butternut squash before, give it a go. It is really delicious and this is a very simple dish to prepare.

PLAN AHEAD
Oven-cook recipe

Serves 4–6

1–2 butternut squash

Olive oil

Sprinkling of paprika

Seasoning to taste

1 red onion, finely chopped

2–3 garlic cloves, crushed

1 chilli, deseeded and finely chopped

1–2 tsp curry powder

1 red pepper, deseeded and finely chopped

400g tin of chopped tomatoes

400g tin of mixed beans, drained

Small handful of fresh coriander leaves, finely chopped

Grated cheese, (optional; omit if vegan)

1 Preheat the oven to 190°C (gas mark 5).

2 While the oven is preheating, halve the butternut squash and remove the seeds. Using a sharp knife, score the flesh of the butternut squash in a criss-cross pattern.

3 Place the squash on a greased baking tray, cut side up. Brush with olive oil and a sprinkling of paprika.

4 Place in the oven and bake for 20 minutes.

5 While the squash is cooking, in a sauté pan, fry the onion, garlic and chilli until they start to soften. Add the curry powder and red pepper and cook for another couple of minutes before adding all the remaining ingredients, apart from the cheese (if using).

6   Cook for another 5 minutes, making sure the ingredients are well combined, then leave to one side until needed.

7   When the butternut squash is soft, remove it from the oven. Scoop out a little of the flesh to form a small well in the centre of each half of the butternut squash. Add this flesh to the bean mixture.

8   Spoon the bean mixture onto the butternut squash. If you like cheesy chilli flavours, you can scatter grated cheese over the top before placing back in the oven for 10–15 minutes until golden.

9   Serve with a green salad.

Vegetable and Bean Crumble

This is a very filling one-pot dish, packed with goodness, and it's also a good way of using up any odd vegetables you have in the fridge.

PLAN AHEAD
Oven-cook recipe
Double up
and freeze

Serves 4–6

1 sweet potato, diced

1 white potato, diced

1 carrot, diced

Olive oil

1 onion, finely chopped

2–3 garlic cloves, finely chopped

1 red pepper, deseeded and diced

1 stick of celery, diced

1 tin of chopped tomatoes

200ml vegetable stock

1 tin of mixed beans

1–2 handfuls of baby leaf spinach

Small handful of mixed fresh herbs

Seasoning to taste

175g plain flour

75g butter (if vegan, use vegan spread)

50g mature Cheddar (if vegan, omit the cheese or substitute with a sprinkling of nutritional yeast flakes or vegan cheese)

1   Prepare the vegetables. Place the potatoes and carrots in a steamer and steam for 10 minutes to help soften.

2   Meanwhile, heat a splash of olive oil in a sauté pan and cook the onion and garlic until it starts to soften. Add the pepper, celery, chopped tomatoes, vegetable stock, beans, spinach and herbs and cook for 10 minutes.

3   Preheat the oven to 180°C (gas mark 4).

4   Add the potatoes and carrots to the tomato mixture and season to taste. Pour this into a deep ovenproof dish.

5   Place the flour in a bowl and rub in the butter to form a texture
    similar to breadcrumbs. Add the grated cheese (if using) and season.

6   Sprinkle the breadcrumb mixture over the vegetable base. You can
    leave this to cool and freeze, leave in the fridge until ready to cook
    or place immediately into your preheated oven and cook for 20
    minutes, until golden and bubbling.

7   Serve on its own or with a salad for a perfect meal.

Spicy Spinach and Potato

I love this dish and it is perfect for using up any cooked potatoes from the night before. You can turn the basic recipe into several different variations, depending on what you fancy!

PLAN AHEAD
Hob recipe
Double up
and freeze

Serves 4

1–2 tbsp olive oil

1 onion, chopped

2 garlic cloves, crushed

2 tsp turmeric

2–3 tsp curry paste

4–5 potatoes, cooked and diced

300g spinach leaves

1   Place the oil, onion and garlic in a pan and cook until the onion and garlic have softened. Add the turmeric and curry paste; cook for another minute.

2   Add the cooked potato. If the mixture looks too dry, add a little water. Stir to ensure that the potato is well coated in spices.

3   Place the spinach in a colander and rinse with hot water for a few seconds to wilt the leaves, then add to the potato mixture and stir well. You can also use frozen spinach for this – simply add the chunks and cook until they are soft.

4   Mix well to make sure everything has a thorough coating of spices. Serve while hot, or cool to freeze.

Extra Recipes

*Make **Spicy Spinach and Potato Pasties** by wrapping balls of the mixture in light wholemeal pastry and cooking for 25–30 mins at 180°C (gas mark 4). Make **Spicy Spinach and Potato Samosas**, by wrapping any leftovers in filo pastry and cooking for 20 mins at 180°C (gas mark 4). Either option would be a delicious addition to a packed lunch or picnic, or would make a tasty snack. Or add a tin of chickpeas to the recipe to make a delicious **Spicy Chickpea, Spinach and Potato Curry** to eat as a side dish with other curries or as a complete meal.*

Mushroom and Cashew Nut Roast

This is a fantastic recipe for a roast or Christmas dinner and it's popular with meat eaters and vegetarians alike. It really speeds up the preparation process if you have a food processor.

PLAN AHEAD

Oven-cook recipe
Double up
and freeze

Serves 6

1 tbsp olive oil	250g mushrooms, finely chopped)
1 large onion, finely chopped	2 tsp yeast extract
200g cashew nuts, chopped	50g breadcrumbs (page 12)

1   Preheat the oven to 180°C (gas mark 4).

2   Fry the onion in the oil until it is translucent.

3   Add the nuts and mushrooms and cook for 5 minutes.

4   Add the yeast extract, followed by the breadcrumbs. Mix well and tip into a loaf tin, greased and lined with baking parchment.

5   Press down the mixture to push it into the corners of the tin and to make sure it is firm. Bake in the oven for 40 minutes.

Storage Tip

I freeze my nut roast in the loaf tin before baking, then tip it out and put it in a freezer bag for storage. It's ready to pop back in the tin whenever I want to cook it, but my loaf tin isn't stuck in the freezer, so I can still use it for other recipes.

Cooking Tip

I prefer chestnut mushrooms in this dish, but choose whatever works for you.

Extra Recipes

*Wrap the mixture in puff pastry to make a **Mushroom en Croute**, which looks very impressive, particularly for Christmas lunch or as an alternative to meat when putting together a roast. Roll the pastry out on a floured surface and place on a baking tray. Spoon the mixture in the middle along the length of the pastry and, using a sharp knife, cut 3–4-cm strips either side of the mixture. Fold these over the mixture to form a pleated effect, then brush with beaten egg or milk and bake at 200°C (gas mark 6) for 40 minutes, until golden.*

Moroccan-style Vegetable Tagine with Quinoa

This is a wholesome dish with a kick. Serve with quinoa as this is much better nutritionally than the traditional couscous.

PLAN AHEAD

Slow cooker recipe
Double up
and freeze

Serves 4–6

1 red onion, diced

2–3 garlic cloves, roughly chopped

1 chilli, finely chopped

2cm piece of fresh ginger, finely chopped

2 peppers, deseeded and diced

2 carrots, diced

2 sweet potatoes, diced

1 white potato, peeled and diced

400g tin of chopped tomatoes

400g tin of chickpeas, drained

40g dried apricots, halved

1–2 tsp chilli powder

½ tsp chilli flakes (optional)

2 tsp turmeric

½ tsp ground cinnamon

½ tsp dried mint

½ tsp ground coriander

200ml hot water

Freshly chopped coriander and flaked almonds (for garnish)

1   If your slow cooker needs to be preheated, turn it on 15 minutes before using. Refer to your manufacturer's instructions for more information on your specific model temperatures.

2   Put all the ingredients in the slow cooker. Make sure the stock is hot when adding as this will keep the temperature high.

3   Turn the slow cooker to low and cook gently for 8–10 hours.

4   Serve with quinoa and a garnish of freshly chopped coriander and flaked almonds.

Healthy Tip

Quinoa is a complete protein that will keep you feeling full for longer than other carbohydrates, helping you with weight loss. It has also been shown to protect against some cancers, particularly in pre-menopausal women. It contains more iron than other grains and is a very good source of fibre and potassium, as well as being a rich source of vitamin E.

Vegetable Curry

This is a great dish to use up any odd bits of vegetables you have lurking in the bottom of your fridge. If you don't have yellow split peas, use red lentils. Both add bulk and additional nutrients while keeping costs low.

PLAN AHEAD
Hob recipe
Double up
and freeze

Serves 4

1–2 tbsp olive oil

1 large onion, finely chopped

2–3 garlic cloves, crushed

3cm piece of fresh ginger, thinly sliced

2–3 tbsp medium curry paste

1 chilli, deseeded and chopped (optional)

1 red pepper, deseeded and chopped

4 ripe tomatoes, chopped and skinned (if preferred)

1 sweet potato, cubed

1 large white potato, cubed

150g yellow split peas

500ml water

2 handfuls of baby leaf spinach

Handful of fresh coriander, roughly shredded

1   Heat the oil in a large casserole or deep sauté pan, then fry the onion, garlic and ginger for a couple of minutes to soften before adding the curry paste and chilli. This can give off quite a fierce aroma so don't lean right over the pan! If the mixture looks dry, add a splash of water.

2   Add the pepper, tomatoes and potatoes. Stir together and simmer gently for 5 minutes.

3   Add the split peas and water. Cover the pan with a lid and simmer gently on a medium heat for 20 minutes until the vegetables are soft.

4   Stir in the spinach and coriander and cook for a further 5 minutes before serving. If freezing, cool first.

Spinach and Ricotta Lasagne

This dish has some fantastic flavours, so even if you aren't vegetarian, give it a try as I am sure it will impress.

PLAN AHEAD

Oven-cook recipe
**Double up
and freeze**

Serves 4–6

1 onion, finely chopped	Black pepper to taste
250g pot ricotta	6–8 sheets of lasagne
100g mature Cheddar, grated	350g jar of tomato pasta sauce
150g fresh spinach leaves (baby spinach is best)	A little Parmesan or other hard cheese, for topping
Grated nutmeg	

1 Place the onion, ricotta and Cheddar in a bowl and mix together well. Put the spinach in a colander and rinse with hot tap a few seconds to wilt the leaves,. Add to the cheese and onion and combine well.

2 Once mixed, add some grated nutmeg and season with black pepper.

3 Place a thin layer of the ricotta mixture in the base of a lasagne dish, followed by a layer of lasagne sheets. Top with a layer of pasta sauce.

4 Continue with a layer of ricotta, then lasagne, and finally the remaining pasta sauce. Add approximately 30ml water to the empty jar, rinse the jar and pour the water over the top of the lasagne.

5 Grate the Parmesan over the lasagne. Season with black pepper.

6 You can freeze the dish at this point, or bake it immediately in a preheated oven at 190°C (gas mark 5) for 40–45 minutes.

7 Serve with **Homemade Potato Wedges** (page 61) and salad.

DESSERTS

Putting this chapter together has certainly been a trip back in time. I don't tend to make desserts every day, but when I was a child we always had a pudding with every evening meal. My parents had an allotment and we had lots of seasonal fruit, which Mum also used to freeze. We used to pick the windfalls from the orchard of my uncle's farm, too, and then spend a good few hours peeling, chopping and bagging them ready for the freezer. With our cold, wet hands, we hated it at the time, but we certainly loved the puddings and cakes Mum created for us all year round. Dad still doesn't think the meal is complete until he has had his pudding!

Many of these recipes can be prepared in advance. Some can be frozen. So, remember to follow the golden rule – double up the recipe and freeze one to always be one step ahead and create your very own ready-meals, or if you have the oven on for another recipe, fill it up with either a dessert, cakes, biscuits or treats for the week ahead.

Chocolate, Pear and Hazelnut Betty

I use tinned pears, but if you prefer fresh, poach them gently for 20 minutes before adding to the recipe.

PLAN AHEAD
Oven-cook recipe
Double up
and freeze

Serves 4–6

420g tin of pears, sliced, including the natural fruit juice

125g breadcrumbs (page 12)

50g oats

50g chopped hazelnuts

75g dark chocolate chunks

2 tsp ground cinnamon

100g butter

3 tbsp golden syrup

1   Preheat the oven to 190°C (gas mark 5).

2   Place the pear slices, with their juice, in an ovenproof dish.

3   Combine the breadcrumbs, oats, chopped hazelnuts, chocolate chunks and cinnamon. Arrange the mixture over the top of the pears.

4   Place the butter and syrup in a small saucepan and melt over a low heat, stirring with a wooden spoon to avoid burning. Once melted, pour over the breadcrumb mixture.

5   Bake in the oven for 15–20 minutes until golden.

6   Serve with a dollop of crème fraîche or vanilla ice-cream.

Gooseberry Betty

This wonderfully satisfying dessert is a great variation to the standard fruit crumble. You can use frozen gooseberries if you prefer.

PLAN AHEAD

Oven-cook recipe
Double up
and freeze

Serves 4–6

750g gooseberries	50g oats
1–2 tbsp sugar	2 tsp ground cinnamon
1–2 tbsp water	100g butter
125g breadcrumbs (page 12)	3 tbsp golden syrup

1   Preheat the oven to 190°C (gas mark 5).

2   Place the gooseberries in a saucepan with the sugar and water then cook over a medium heat for 5 minutes to help them soften. Stir and press the gooseberries slightly to encouraage them to burst a little. Tip them into an ovenproof dish when they are ready.

3   While the gooseberries are cooking, combine the breadcrumbs, oats and cinnamon in a bowl. Spread this mixture over the top of the fruit.

4   Place the butter and syrup in a saucepan and melt very gently, stirring with a wooden spoon to avoid burning. Once melted, pour over the breadcrumb mixture. You can freeze at this point for use later.

5   Bake for 15–20 minutes, until the top is golden.

6   Serve with a dollop of crème fraîche or vanilla ice-cream.

--- **Top Tip** ---

May be frozen cooked or uncooked. If heating from frozen, add 10 minutes to the cooking time. The food is ready when it is piping hot throughout.

Raspberry Brûlée

This is a delicious dessert that takes minutes to prepare. My dad loves making this as it gives him an excuse to get out his kitchen blowtorch and makes him feel like a celebrity chef!

PLAN AHEAD
No cook

Serves 4–6

200g frozen raspberries (or fresh ones if they are in season)

350–400g fat-free Greek yoghurt

3 tbsp low-fat crème fraîche

1 tsp vanilla paste

3–4 tbsp brown sugar

1   If you are using frozen raspberries, place them in a heatproof serving dish and allow them to defrost for 20 minutes. You could use individual serving dishes, as long as they are heatproof.

2   Meanwhile, mix the yoghurt and crème fraîche together in a bowl. Once combined, add the vanilla paste and stir well.

3   Spoon the yoghurt mixture over the raspberries, then sprinkle with brown sugar – enough to form a generous layer to make the crème brûlée effect.

4   You can use a kitchen blowtorch to caramelise the top or place the dish under a hot grill. Be sure to watch this stage carefully, as the sugar can caramelise really quickly and could burn if you are not paying attention. Serve immediately.

Lemon Saucy Pudding

This is a deceptively light pudding that is really quite addictive. My mum used to make it for us when we were children and it is now a favourite with my boys. The soufflé-like sponge sits on top of a zingy lemon sauce. You can use fewer lemons if you prefer a less intense citrus hit.

PLAN AHEAD
Oven-cook recipe

Serves 4–6

50g butter, plus extra for greasing

150g sugar

Zest and juice of 2 large or 3 medium lemons

4 medium eggs (or 3 large), separated

1 tsp vanilla essence or paste

50g plain flour

300ml milk

1   Preheat the oven to 180°C (gas mark 4) and butter a baking dish or individual ramekins, if you prefer.

2   In a bowl, beat the butter and sugar together until creamy, then add the lemon zest.

3   Add the egg yolks, vanilla and lemon juice. Beat well, then add the flour and milk to form a batter. Mix well, scraping down the edges of the bowl.

4   In a clean bowl, beat the egg whites until they form soft peaks. Fold into the batter, taking care to avoid over-stirring, as you want to keep the air in the egg whites.

5   Pour the mixture into the baking dish. You can keep it in the fridge at this stage if you want to bake it later.

6   Boil a kettle of water. Place the baking dish in a roasting tray and place this in the oven. Pour the boiling water into the tray to create

a *bain marie.* but don't splash any water onto the pudding! I find it far easier and safer to do this while the dish is in the oven as it avoids carrying and spilling the hot water.

7   Bake for 30 minutes (20 minutes for individual ramekin portions). The pudding will have a golden sponge topping which is firm to the touch and a gooey lemon sauce beneath it.

8   Serve with crème fraîche or Greek yoghurt.

Baked Bananas with Dark Chocolate Sauce

Wow, what a combination! Bananas and dark chocolate with crème fraîche.

PLAN AHEAD
Oven-cook recipe

Serves 4

4 bananas
100–150g dark chocolate

4 heaped dessertspoons crème fraîche

1   Preheat the oven to 180°C (gas mark 4).

2   Place the bananas in an ovenproof dish in their skins and bake for 10 minutes, or until the skin goes completely black. When the bananas are cooked, remove from their skins.

3   Meanwhile, melt the dark chocolate in a heat-resistant bowl set over a pan of just-simmering water.

4   Pour the chocolate over the bananas when you are ready to serve and finish with a generous dollop of crème fraîche.

Chocolate Saucy Pudding

The sauce is poured over the top of the cake, but during cooking the sauce miraculously goes to the bottom. Magic!

PLAN AHEAD
Oven-cook recipe

Serves 4–6

115g sugar, plus 2 tbsp	100g self-raising flour
115g butter, plus extra for greasing	2 tbsp cocoa
2 eggs, beaten	300ml boiling water
2 tbsp milk	2 tbsp sugar
1 tbsp vanilla essence or paste	1 tbsp cocoa

1   Preheat the oven to 180°C (gas mark 4).

2   Beat the sugar and butter together in a bowl until creamy and fluffy. Gradually add the beaten eggs, milk and vanilla. Mix well before adding the flour and cocoa.

3   Pour into a greased ovenproof dish (or ramekin dishes) and smooth over with a palette knife to flatten.

4   In a bowl or jug, combine the boiling water, 2 tablespoons sugar and cocoa. Stir well until there are no lumps. Pour this over the sponge mixture.

5   Bake for 25–30 minutes, until the sponge is firm to the touch.

6   Serve with a dollop of Greek yoghurt, crème fraîche or **Homemade Custard** (page 199).

Cooking Tip

Use ramekins to make individual puddings for a party. Simply bake in the oven for 15-20 minutes.

Simple Cheat's Eccles Cakes

These were my dad's favourite when I was growing up. They don't last long in our home!

PLAN AHEAD
Oven-cook recipe
Packed lunches and picnics
Double up
and freeze

Makes 6–8 cakes, depending on size

Flour for rolling out

250g pack of puff pastry

4 tbsp mincemeat

1 egg, beaten

Sprinkling of brown sugar

1   Preheat the oven to 200°C (gas mark 6).

2   On a floured surface, roll the pastry out to about 4–5mm thick and cut into squares, approximately 15–20cm square.

3   Place 2–3 teaspoons of mincemeat in the centre of each pastry square.

4   Using a pastry brush, brush beaten egg around the edges of each square. Then fold the corners into the centre to form an envelope and gather in the remaining folds to make a bundle. Or simply fold over and secure to form a rectangle or a triangle.

5   On a floured surface, turn the cakes over so that the seams are on the bottom. Use a rolling pin or your hands to gently flatten the cakes slightly, being careful not to split the pastry.

6   Using a sharp knife, score 2–3 slits in the top of each cake. Place on a baking tray and brush with beaten egg and a sprinkling of brown sugar before placing in the oven. Bake for 15 minutes until golden.

--- Top Tip ---

May be frozen cooked or uncooked. If heating from frozen, add 10 minutes to the cooking time. The food is ready when it is piping hot throughout. Check and if it is not ready, pop back into the oven for another five minutes, then check again.

Fruit Compôte

This versatile dessert is equally delicious as a pudding at a dinner party, or used the next day as a topping on your breakfast porridge. The recipe can be adapted to use up whatever fruits you have left over in your fridge: oranges, pears, peaches are particularly good!

PLAN AHEAD
Hob recipe
Double up
and freeze

Serves 4

400g mixed berries (such as blackberries, blueberries, raspberries, redcurrants)

1 large apple, peeled, cored and chopped roughly

2 large plums, skinned and chopped roughly

2 teaspoons of lemon juice

2 tablespoons of water

25g sugar (optional)

1 cinnamon stick (for a slightly spicy flavour)

1   Mix the ingredients in a saucepan and bring to the boil. Allow to simmer over a low heat for 3-5 minutes, stirring occasionally to prevent the mixture from sticking.

2   Take off the heat, remove the cinnamon stick, and spoon the mix-

ture into 4 heat-proof dessert bowls or brandy glasses. Add a dollop of crème fraîche and serve immediately with a biscuit like **Viennese Whirls** (page 232).

— **Storage Tip** —

Seal in a container in the fridge for up to 2 days. Alternatively, freeze individual portions and defrost before re-heating for a few minutes. Will keep in the freezer for up to 3 months.

Apple and Cinnamon Cobbler

You can adjust the amount of cinnamon here to suit your own taste.

PLAN AHEAD
Oven-cook recipe
Double up
and freeze

Serves 4–6

3–4 Bramley cooking apples, peeled, cored and chopped

1–2 tbsp brown sugar (depending on desired sweetness)

1–2 tsp ground cinnamon

Juice of half a lemon

50g raisins

150g self-raising flour, plus extra for rolling out

½ tsp baking powder

25g sugar

50g butter

100ml natural yoghurt

1 tsp vanilla essence

Milk, for glazing

1   Preheat the oven to 190°C (gas mark 5).

2   Place the apples, brown sugar, cinnamon, lemon and raisins in a saucepan and add the water. Cook on a medium heat until the apples start to soften.

3   To make the scones, sift the flour into a bowl and add the baking powder and sugar. Rub in the butter with your fingertips until the mixture resembles breadcrumbs.

4   Add the yoghurt and vanilla essence and mix to form a dough. Then turn out the dough onto a floured surface, roll into a thick sausage then cut into 4–5cm rounds.

5   Tip the apple mixture into an ovenproof dish and arrange the scones around the edge and over the top. Brush with milk and add a sprinkling of brown sugar. If freezing, do it at this point. Otherwise bake for 15–18 minutes, until golden.

6   Serve with **Homemade Custard** (page 199).

Top Tip

May be frozen cooked or uncooked. If heating from frozen, add 10 minutes to the cooking time. The food is ready when it is piping hot throughout. Check and if it is not ready, pop back into the oven for another five minutes, then check again.

Homemade Custard

Although it takes a little more care than powdered custard, the result of making your own from scratch is spectacular.

PLAN AHEAD
Hob recipe
Double up
and freeze

Serves 4

600ml full fat milk	3 tbsp sugar
4 egg yolks	1 tsp vanilla essence
4 tbsp cornflour	

1　Heat the milk to just below boiling point. Meanwhile, mix the egg yolks, cornflour and sugar together. Keep an eye on the milk to avoid it boiling over. Add the vanilla essence.

2　Remove the milk from the heat and add the egg mixture. Use a hand whisk and stir well.

3　Place the custard back on the heat and continue to stir until it starts to thicken – be careful not to have the heat too high or it will burn.

4　Once the custard has thickened, serve immediately.

Leftover Tip

If you have any custard left over, you could pour this into lolly moulds and freeze – these make delicious ice-lollies!

Queen of Puddings

Comforting puddings like this are enjoying a well-deserved revival and are so much nicer than shop-bought, processed puddings.

PLAN AHEAD

Oven-cook recipe

Serves 4–6

90g white bread, cubed

45g sugar

420ml milk

1 tsp vanilla extract or paste

45g butter, plus extra for greasing

2 eggs, separated

3 tbsp jam (I use raspberry but feel free to use whatever you prefer)

60g caster sugar

1   Preheat the oven to 180°C (gas mark 4) butter an ovenproof dish.

2   Place the cubed bread in a bowl and sprinkle with the sugar.

3   Heat the milk, vanilla extract or paste and butter in a saucepan until it almost reaches boiling point and then pour over the bread and sugar mixture. When this is cool, add the egg yolks and whisk until smooth.

4   Pour the mixture into your greased, ovenproof dish and bake for 20–25 minutes, until set.

5   While this is cooking, in a bowl beat the egg whites until they form soft peaks, gradually adding half the caster sugar.

6   Melt the jam over a low heat so that it does not burn, then spread it over the set bread pudding mixture.

7   Top with the whisked egg whites, sprinkle with the remaining caster sugar and return the pudding to the oven for another 8–10 minutes, until golden.

8   Serve with **Homemade Custard** (page 199)

Leftover Tip

You can also make this with panettone or any fruit loaf that has gone stale.

Baked Cinnamon Apples

A traditional autumnal treat that is simple to prepare. No mince-meat? Then fill the apples with dried fruit and honey.

PLAN AHEAD
Oven recipe

Serves 4

4 Bramley apples	4 tbsp mincemeat
2 tsp runny honey	Sprinkling of brown sugar
2–3 tsp ground cinnamon	

1   Preheat the oven to 200°C (gas mark 6).

2   Wash and core your apples, leaving the skins intact. Mix the honey with 2 teaspoons of boiling water and the cinnamon. Stir until dissolved.

3   Place the apples on a baking tray and add 2 tablespoons of water to the dish. Brush the apples with the honey mixture.

4   Fill the cores of the apples with mincemeat, then finish off with a sprinkling of brown sugar.

5   Bake in the oven for 20–30 minutes until soft and serve with low-fat crème fraîche, natural yoghurt, or **Homemade Custard** (page 199).

Apple and Date Bread and Butter Pudding

A twist on a traditional favourite. I can normally create this just from what I have in my store cupboard.

PLAN AHEAD
Oven-cook recipe
Double up
and freeze

Serves 4–6

4–6 slices of white bread (stale is ideal)

30g butter, plus extra for greasing

40g chopped dates

1 cooking apple, peeled and chopped

50g sugar

2 tsp ground cinnamon, plus extra for sprinkling (optional)

2 eggs, beaten

300ml milk

75ml cream (optional – increase the quantity of milk to 375ml if you prefer)

1   Preheat the oven to 190°C (gas mark 5). Butter an ovenproof dish.

2   Butter the bread and use to line the dish, sprinkling chopped dates, chopped apple, sugar and cinnamon between the slices.

3   In a jug, whisk together the eggs, milk and cream (if used). Pour over the bread mixture, pushing the bread down into the liquid where necessary. Let it sit for 10 minutes to absorb the milk.

4   Sprinkle the pudding with more cinnamon (optional) and place the dish in the oven, or you can freeze at this point, if you prefer.

5   Bake for 30 minutes, until golden and the base is almost set.

6   Serve with **Homemade Custard** (page 199).

Cooking Tip

No dates in your kitchen cupboard? Then just use sultanas, instead.

Leftover Tip

This recipe is perfect for using up any bread that is going stale.

Pear and Dark Chocolate Granola Layer

You can use a plain granola and mix in your own dark chocolate chips, or look out for a chocolate granola mix in the shops.

PLAN AHEAD
Oven-cook recipe
Double up
and freeze

Serves 4

8–12 tbsp granola (you can use muesli)

75g dark chocolate chips (if you are not using dark chocolate granola)

2 tbsp chopped hazelnuts

400g tinned pears in natural juice, sliced

1 Preheat the oven to 180°C (gas mark 4.)

2 Mix the granola, chocolate chips and hazelnuts together in a bowl.

3 Spoon half the pears and their juice into an ovenproof dish. Cover with a layer of granola mix, then repeat with another layer of pears and granola. You can freeze at this point for use later.

4 Place in the oven and bake for 15 minutes.

5 Serve hot or cold with either ice cream, freshly whipped cream, or **Homemade Custard** (page 199).

Pineapple Upside-down Cake

A traditional family favourite that can be a pudding or a cake, as it may be served hot or cold. This recipe also works well with apricots.

PLAN AHEAD
Oven-cook recipe
Packed lunch
Double up
and freeze

Serves 4–6

150g butter, plus extra for greasing

150g sugar

3 eggs, beaten

150g self-raising flour, sifted

1 tsp vanilla essence

50g butter

50g brown sugar

2 tbsp golden syrup

1 tin pineapple rings

3 glacé cherries, halved

1 Preheat the oven to 180°C (gas mark 4).

2 In a bowl, beat together the butter and sugar until golden and creamy. Gradually add the eggs and combine well.

3 Fold in the sifted flour and once combined, add the vanilla essence.

4 Place the butter, brown sugar and golden syrup in a heat-resistant bowl and set this over a pan of gently simmering water to melt the butter. Stir gently with a wooden spoon to avoid burning. You can do this in a microwave on low power, but keep a close eye on it.

5 Grease or line an ovenproof dish or cake tin. Place a small amount of the buttery syrup mixture into the dish then lay the pineapple rings in the bottom with a cherry in the middle of the each one. Pour over the remaining melted buttery, syrup mixture.

6 Carefully spoon over the sponge mix to cover the pineapple rings and smooth the surface with a spatula or palette knife.

7   Place in the oven and bake for 20–25 minutes, until the sponge is risen, golden and springs back into shape when pressed.

8   Remove from the oven and leave to rest for a few minutes. Place a plate or serving dish over the top of the dish and flip it over so the cake sits on the plate, upside down, with the pineapple facing upwards.

9   Serve with a dollop of crème fraîche or **Homemade Custard** (page 199)

Leftover Tip

Freeze this cake after baking. Defrost it at room temperature and reheat in the oven on a low temperature (160°C/gas mark 3) for 10 minutes before serving.

Cheat's Ginger and Apple Layer

Such a simple dish, using some store-cupboard staples. Thrown together in minutes, it is perfect for a quick and easy dessert.

PLAN AHEAD

Oven-cook recipe

Serves 4–6

700g bramley apples, cored, peeled and diced

2 tbsp water

50g brown sugar, plus 1 tbsp for sprinkling

50g sultanas

1 tsp cinnamon

Butter for greasing

1 small ginger cake, crumbled

Zest and juice of one orange

1 tbsp desiccated coconut

1   Place the chopped apple in a saucepan with the water and brown sugar. Cook until it starts to soften, but still has a bite. Add the sultanas and cinnamon and combine well.

2   Preheat the oven to 180°C (gas mark 4) and meanwhile, grease an ovenproof dish.

3   Crumble a layer of ginger cake in the bottom of the ovenproof dish. Over this, add a layer of apple. Repeat, finishing with a ginger cake top.

4   Add the orange zest and juice. Sprinkle with coconut and 1 tablespoon of brown sugar. Bake in the oven for 15 minutes.

5   Serve with **Homemade Custard** (page199) or **Butterscotch Sauce** (page 207).

Cooking Tip

*Cook up a batch of stewed apple and keep it in a sealed
container in the fridge for up to 3 days. Alternatively, store
stewed apple or raw sliced apple in the freezer ready to be heated
to use in pies, crumbles or puddings.*

Leftover Tip

*If you have some ginger cake left, you can serve this with
tinned mandarin oranges and custard for a very easy extra
dessert.*

Butterscotch Sauce

This is a very sweet treat to drizzle over ice-cream or other puddings
– you only nteed a small amount to make a delicious difference.

PLAN AHEAD
Hob recipe

Serves 4

60g butter	6 tbsp golden syrup
120g brown sugar	6 tbsp double cream

1   Place the butter, brown sugar and golden syrup in a saucepan and
    melt gently over a low heat, so that it does not burn. Stir well to
    combine.

2   Fold in the double cream (single cream may curdle or separate).

3   Serve hot or cold with baked desserts or over ice-cream.

Apple, Sultana and Cinnamon Pie

This dish uses a sweet pastry but you will not lose anything if you opt for a traditional pastry. You can, of course, use readymade pastry.

PLAN AHEAD
Oven-cook recipe
Packed lunches and picnics
Double up
and freeze

Serves 6–8

250g plain flour, plus extra for rolling out

75g caster sugar or icing sugar

Zest and juice of 1 orange

125g butter

1kg cooking apples, peeled, cored and sliced

Ground cinnamon

50g sultanas

75g sugar, plus extra for sprinkling

1 egg, beaten, for glazing

1   Preheat the oven to 190°C (gas mark 5).

2   To make the pastry, it is easiest to use a food processor. Add the flour, caster or icing sugar, orange zest and butter to the bowl. Whizz for a couple of seconds. Slowly add the orange juice until a dough forms. Place the dough in the fridge to rest for 5 minutes.

3   Roll the pastry out onto a floured board to the desired size and thickness for your 25cm pie dish. You will need to line the pie dish and have enough pastry for a lid.

4   Press the pastry firmly around the bottom of the dish and the sides, then use a knife to trim away any excess.

5   Cover the pastry base with baking parchment and baking beans. Bake blind for 10 minutes, then remove the beans and parchment and return to the oven for another 8–10 minutes, until golden.

6 Arrange the apple slices in the pie dish, layering with cinnamon and sultanas. Sprinkle over the sugar. Brush some beaten egg over the edges of the pastry base to help secure the lid, then place the pastry top over the pie base and crimp the edges to seal them. You can freeze at this point for use later.

7 Brush the top with beaten egg and sprinkle with sugar before placing in the oven for 30–40 minutes, until golden.

8 Serve with a dollop of crème fraîche or low-fat yoghurt.

Extra Recipes

Double up the recipe but instead of adding a pastry top, sprinkle some Oaty Crumble Mix (page 210) over the top of the apples. A fantastic variation to this recipe with very little effort!

Apple and Blackberry Pie

A classic, delicious autumnal pie that makes the most of freshly picked blackberries and seasonal apples.

PLAN AHEAD
Oven-cook recipe
Packed lunches and picnics
Double up
and freeze

Serves 6–8

250g plain flour

75g caster sugar or icing sugar

125g butter

1 egg, beaten

1kg cooking apples, peeled, cored and sliced

200g blackberries

75g sugar

1 Preheat the oven to 190°C (gas mark 5).

2 To make the pastry, it is easiest to use a food processor. Add the flour, caster or icing sugar and butter to the bowl. Whizz for a couple of seconds. Slowly add the egg until a dough forms. You may use only half the egg, set aside whatever remains to glaze the pie. Place the dough in the fridge to rest for 5 minutes.

3 Roll the pastry out onto a floured board to the desired size and thickness for your 25cm pie dish. You need enough to line and cover the dish.

4 Press the pastry firmly around the bottom of the dish and the sides, then use a knife to trim away any excess.

5 Cover the pastry base with baking parchment and baking beans and bake blind for 10 minutes. Remove the beans and baking parchment and return to the oven for another 8–10 minutes, until golden.

6 Place the apple and blackberries in the pie dish and sprinkle over the sugar. Brush some egg over the edges of the pastry base to help secure the lid, then top the pie with pastry and crimp the edges to seal.

7 Brush the pie with the remaining beaten egg and sprinkle with extra sugar before placing in the oven for 30–40 minutes until golden.

8   Serve with a dollop of crème fraîche, low fat yoghurt or **Homemade Custard** (page 199).

Top Tip

May be frozen cooked or uncooked. If heating from frozen, add 10 minutes to the cooking time. The food is ready when it is piping hot throughout. Check and if it is not ready, pop back into the oven for another five minutes, then check again.

Cooking Tip

I prefer my apples in a pie to have a slight bite to them rather than be a soggy mush, so I tend to put the apples and blackberries straight into the pie. If you prefer, place the apples and blackberries in a pan with a very small amount of water and cook for 10 minutes on a medium heat until soft – then add to the pie.

No-messing Rice Pudding

Most people cook rice pudding in the oven, but I find making it in a saucepan so much easier. For added creaminess, you can use full-fat milk, or stir in some double cream prior to serving.

PLAN AHEAD
Hob recipe
Double up
and freeze

Serves 6

110g pudding rice or arborio risotto rice

750ml full fat milk

150ml double cream

2–3 tsp cinnamon

1–2 tsp pure vanilla extract

25g sugar

A little grated nutmeg to serve

1   Place all the ingredients apart from the double cream and nutmeg in a heavy based saucepan. Make sure this pan is at least a third larger than the contents.

2   On a low heat, cook the rice mixture until it is soft, stirring often to avoid it sticking to the base of your pan. The rice will thicken and soften in about 20 minutes and you may have to add more milk, if necessary, depending on how thick you like your pudding. Remember the pudding does absorb milk after cooking so if reheating, you will need to add more milk.

3   Just before serving, you can stir in some double cream if you like a creamy taste. Transfer to bowls and serve sprinkled with nutmeg or **Fruit Compôte** (page 196–7), or allow to cool before freezing.

Extra Recipes

Raspberry Rice Pudding Brûlée *Place some frozen raspberries in an ovenproof dish (or mini ramekin dishes). Add rice pudding and finish with a sprinkling of brown sugar. Then use a cook's blowtorch to caramelise the top (you can get a similar effect by placing under the grill but it does take longer). Try this with other left-over fruit, too.*

Rhubarb and Ginger Rice Pudding Brûlée *Using the same technique as above, place rhubarb chunks in the base of a ramekin or ovenproof dish. Grate a sprinkling of fresh ginger over the rhubarb – be careful as it can give quite a kick! Cover with rice pudding and sprinkle with brown sugar before caramelising as above.*

Summer Pudding

You can use fresh fruits or frozen berries for this desert if you want to make it out of season. It's my mum's favourite pudding – serve with some clotted cream if you are feeling naughty – and a great way to use up stale bread.

PLAN AHEAD
Hob recipe
Double up
and freeze

Serves 4

500g mixed berries (such as strawberries, raspberries, blueberries, cherries or blackberries – you can use frozen mixed fruit)

75g golden caster sugar
6 slices white bread

1   Place the fruit and sugar in a saucepan and heat very gently for 2–3 minutes, until the sugar has dissolved. Don't overcook – you want the fruit to retain its shape.

2   Remove from the heat, drain off some of the fruit juice and leave to one side.

3   Meanwhile, line a 1.2-litre pudding basin with the bread slices, ensuring there are no gaps and that the edges overlap. Trim as necessary.

4   Spoon the fruit mixture into the basin. Cover with a layer of bread to help seal the top.

5   Place a saucer over the basin, ideally one that fits inside the basin rim, and press down gently. Place a weight on top of the saucer to keep the shape and chill overnight.

6   When you are ready to serve, turn the pudding out onto a serving plate and drizzle with the remaining fruit juice.

7   Serve with crème fraîche or **Homemade Custard** (page 199).

Blackberry and Apple Crumble

There is nothing nicer than the taste of blackberries and apples to tell you autumn is on its way!

PLAN AHEAD
Oven-cook recipe
Double up
and freeze

Serves 4–6

4 cooking apples, ideally Bramley, peeled, cored and cubed

One or two handfuls of blackberries (fresh or frozen)

25g sugar

For the crumble topping

250g plain flour

200g butter

150g brown sugar

50g oats or muesli

1   Preheat the oven to 180°C (gas mark 4).

2   Place the apples in a saucepan with 1–2 tablespoons of water. Cook over a medium heat for 5–8 minutes until they start to soften slightly.

3   Mix in the blackberries and sugar and stir well.

4   In a mixing bowl, add the flour and butter and rub in with your fingertips until the mixture resembles breadcrumbs. Add the brown sugar and oats or muesli; combine well.

5   Transfer the fruit to an ovenproof dish, then sprinkle on the crumble topping, starting at the outside edge and working inwards. At this point you can freeze for later use. Alternatively, bake in the oven for 15 minutes until the crumble is golden and bubbling.

6   Serve with créme fraîche, freshly whipped cream, or **Homemade Custard** (page 199).

Cooking Tip

If you have no brown sugar for the topping, granulated white sugar will do, but brown sugar gives a better flavour and consistency.

Storage Tip

A batch of crumble mix will keep for up to one month in an airtight container in the fridge.

Extra Recipes

There are endless combinations for a good fruit crumble. Go with the seasons and try to use up any spare fruit in your fruit bowl. Here are some more ideas:

Spiced Apple Crumble *After stewing your apple, stir in some nutmeg, cinnamon and mixed spice with a handful of dried fruit.*

Apple and Blackcurrant Crumble *Blackcurrants add a wonderful flavour and vibrant colour. Place the blackcurrants in the saucepan with the apple to stew together.*

Apple and Blueberry Crumble *Blueberries are marketed as a superfood, but really most berries are good for you. Mix fresh or frozen blueberries into the stewed apple; cover with your crumble mix and bake in the oven for 15–20 minutes.*

Gooseberry and Elderflower Crumble *This is one of my favourites. Place prepared gooseberries in a saucepan and add 2 tablespoons of elderflower cordial and 25g sugar. Simmer gently until the gooseberries just start to burst under pressure. Place in an ovenproof dish and cover with your crumble topping.*

Extra Recipes

Summer Fruit Crumble *This is a lovely 'cheat' crumble. All you need is a pack of frozen summer fruits and a pack of own-brand muesli or crumble ingredients. Place the summer fruits in the bottom of an ovenproof dish, add 2 tablespoons of water and a sprinkling of sugar if you have a sweet tooth. Cover with your crumble mix and bake in the oven for 15–20 minutes.*

Rhubarb Crumble *Cook some fresh or frozen rhubarb in a pan with a little water or mix in some fresh strawberries or raspberries for sweetness. Another great combination is* **Rhubarb and Orange Crumble.** *Add some orange segments alongside the rhubarb. Or, if you like things a bit hot, why not try* **Rhubarb and Ginger Crumble?**

Oaty Crumble Mix

This versatile topping has a delicious texture that complements most cooked fruit fillings.

PLAN AHEAD
No cook
Double up
and freeze

Serves 4

100g plain flour	30g oats
30g brown sugar	little brown sugar, for sprinkling
50g butter, slightly softened	

1 Sift the plain flour into a bowl, and add the softened butter.
2 Rub in the butter with your fingertips until the mixture resembles breadcrumbs.

3   Add the brown sugar and oats, and mix well.

4   Use the mixture to top a crumble filling and bake (for oven times, etc, see individual dessert recipes). If you wish, you may freeze the crumble mix for later use, or store it in a sealable container in the fridge, where it will keep for a month.

Apple and Granola Bird's Nest Layer

In the summer months, you can swap the apple for some delicious crushed berries. Measurements vary depending on the size of glass, so simply layer the ingredients up appropriately.

PLAN AHEAD
Oven-cook recipe

Serves 4

2–3 cooking apples, cored, peeled and diced

2 tbsp water

50g brown sugar

Granola

Crème fraîche (or cream, if you prefer)

Dark chocolate, melted, to decorate

1   Place the chopped apple in a saucepan with the water and brown sugar. Heat until the mixture starts to soften, but still has bite. After you have cooked the apples, allow them to cool.

2   In your chosen serving glasses, place a layer of apple, followed by granola, and then the crème fraîche.

3   Repeat this process, finishing with the crème fraîche.

4   Decorate with swirls of melted dark chocolate.

5   Chill in the fridge for 30 minutes before serving.

Lemon and Ginger Cheesecake

If you don't like the ginger base, swap the ginger biscuits for digestives. I usually top it off with fresh raspberries.

PLAN AHEAD
No cook

Serves 4

150g ginger biscuits, crushed
50g butter
1 tub of low-fat soft cheese
Zest and juice of two small lemons

150g Greek yoghurt
150g crème fraîche
50g plain chocolate

1   Place the crushed biscuits in a saucepan with the butter. Stir well over a gentle heat, until the butter has melted and the biscuit crumbs are thoroughly coated.

2   Transfer the biscuit base to a greased 25 cm cheesecake tin with a removeable bottom. Press down the on biscuit crumbs with your fingertips to form a solid base, then place in the fridge to chill.

3   To make the filling, put the soft cheese in a large bowl and beat with a wooden spoon to soften it. Add the zest of both lemons and the juice of one lemon. Add the yoghurt and crème fraîche. Stir well.

4   Taste to check that the filling is lemony enough. If not, add more lemon juice. When you are happy with the mixture, pour it over the biscuit base, spreading it out evenly and smoothly. Then place the cheesecake in the fridge until set.

5   Melt the chocolate in a heat-resistant bowl over a pan of just-simmering water until the chocolate is smooth and runny enough to decorate the top of the cheesecake. Using a spoon, drizzle the chocolate over the cheesecake to form a pattern.

6   Return the cheesecake to the fridge until you are ready to serve.

TREATS

This section is packed full of tasty treats that make a delicious (and nutritionally better) alternative to reaching for a shop-bought chocolate bar – they are perfect for packed lunches or just for pure enjoyment with a cup of tea.

As with all the recipes in this book, always remember the golden rule: if you are turning on your oven, fill it up! So, if you are making a roast or oven dish for a main meal, refer back to this section for some quick and easy treats that you can cook at the same time for the week ahead. Some can be prepared in advance, some can be frozen, so double up the recipe if you can and freeze a batch for another time.

Death by Chocolate Cake

This is my son's favourite cake. A very rich chocolate cake with a thick, rich fudge-like icing, it goes a long way, as even chocoholics struggle to manage more than a fairly small slice!

PLAN AHEAD
Oven-cook recipe
Packed lunches and picnics
Double up
and freeze

Serves 8

75g cocoa

¾ tsp bicarbonate of soda

200ml boiling water

300g golden caster sugar

4 eggs

1 tsp vanilla paste

180ml light olive oil

200g self-raising flour

For the fudge icing

200g dark chocolate (70 per cent cocoa), broken into pieces

40g unsalted butter

100ml milk

50g cocoa

1 tsp vanilla essence

2 tbsp honey

1   Preheat the oven to 180°C (gas mark 4) and grease and line 2 sponge tins.

2   In a heat-resistent bowl, the cocoa and bicarbonate of soda with the boiling water and leave to one side.

3   Meanwhile, beat the sugar and eggs together in another bowl until light and creamy. Add the vanilla paste and olive oil; continue beating well.

4   Add the flour, followed by the cocoa solution. You can continue to beat this, you don't need to fold in. This will form a batter the consistency of double cream. When it is ready, pour the batter into the sponge tins.

5   Bake for 20–30 minutes, until the cakes are firm to the touch and have slightly pulled away from the edges of the tins.

6   Allow the cakes to cool while you make the icing.

7   Put all the icing ingredients in a heat-resistant bowl set over a pan of just simmering water and stir well as they melt together to form a thick chocolate sauce.

8   Once the sponge is completely cool you can freeze or start to add the icing. Place one sponge, flat side up, on your serving plate or cake stand. Spread half the icing mix onto the sponge and place the second layer on top to form a sandwich. (If you prefer, you can fill the middle with standard butter icing and just use the sauce for the top.)

9   Use the remaining icing to cover the top of the sponge. It will set so don't worry if it drips down the sides of the cake.

Leftover Tip

I doubt if you will have any of this cake left after a few days but if you do, it makes a great pudding topped with mandarin oranges and served with custard.

Chocolate Chip Cupcakes with Vanilla Icing

Whip up a batch of these to bake when you have your oven on to cook a main meal. They take minutes to make when you use an electric mixer. You don't have to add icing to the cakes – they are just as delicious without.

PLAN AHEAD
Oven-cook recipe
Packed lunches and picnics
Double up
and freeze

Makes 12 cupcakes

175g unsalted butter	*For the icing*
175g sugar	50g unsalted butter
3 eggs, beaten	100g cream cheese
150g self-raising flour	200–275g icing sugar
50g plain chocolate chips (can use white if you want a change)	1 tsp vanilla essence or paste
	Sprinkling of chocolate chips or grated chocolate, to decorate

1 Preheat the oven to 200°C (gas mark 6).

2 In a bowl, cream the butter and sugar together until pale and fluffy. Then add the eggs a little at a time and continue to beat well.

3 Sift the flour before gently folding into the mixture. When thoroughly mixed, add the chocolate chips and combine.

4 Spoon the mixture into cupcake or muffin cases in a muffin or cupcake tray and bake for 12–15 minutes. The cakes should be firm and spring back when touched.

5 Cool the cakes on a wire rack. You can freeze at this point, if you prefer.

6 To make the icing, beat the butter and cream cheese together in a bowl until soft.

7   Gradually add the icing sugar and vanilla essence and beat until the mixture is glossy, thick and lump-free.

8   Spoon the icing into an icing bag and fold down the ends to secure. Keep the folded ends of the bag in your fist and gently push down with your hand in a controlled fashion. Start at the outer edge of a cake and spiral inwards covering the whole of the cake top, gently overlapping to avoid gaps. Finish with a sprinkle of chocolate chips or grated chocolate.

Cooking Tip

The best test to check see if you have added enough icing sugar is by tasting it. It should taste sweet and creamy but not too buttery. If you have added too much icing and end up with a dry mix, simply add a dash of milk and re-beat.

Storage Tip

If you have any leftover icing, store it in an airtight container in the fridge, where it should keep for over a week. You may need to add a little milk and re-beat to soften it before use.

Fruit Scones

Buttermilk is the key to light and fluffy scones and these are completely foolproof. I used this recipe to teach primary school children how to cook and even with them overhandling the dough, they all came out perfectly.

PLAN AHEAD

Oven-cook recipe
Packed lunches and picnics
Double up
and freeze

Makes 6–8 scones

250g self-raising flour, plus extra for rolling out

50g butter, plus extra for greasing

50g sugar

50g sultanas, raisins or mixed fruit

1 egg beaten (plus another beaten egg, to glaze)

100ml buttermilk

1   Preheat the oven to 200°C (gas mark 6) and lightly grease a baking tray.

2   Sift the flour into a bowl, add the butter and rub in until the mixture resembles breadcrumbs. Add the sugar and dried fruit and combine well.

3   In another bowl, mix the egg and the buttermilk together and gradually add this to the dry ingredients to form a dough that is firm, but not wet.

4   Tip the dough onto a floured board, and press out with your hands until it is 5cm thick. Cut out 6–8 pastry circles of pastry dough with a pastry cutter and place on the baking tray. Brush with beaten egg. You can freeze at this point, or cook, then freeze once cooled.

5   Place in the oven for 12–18 minutes until golden, then cool on a wire rack.

Top Tip

May be frozen cooked or uncooked. If heating from frozen, add 10 minutes to the cooking time. The food is ready when it is piping hot throughout. Check and if it is not ready, pop back into the oven for another five minutes, then check again.

Storage Tip

Most buttermilk containers in the supermarket are 300ml so you will have some left: either scale up the recipe or freeze the buttermilk. Buttermilk will separate when frozen, so once defrosted make sure you give it a thorough whisk before using.

Extra Recipes

Double this recipe and swap the dried fruit for blueberries in one batch, or make some plain scones that can be eaten as a sweet or savoury.

Cooking Tip

When cutting out the scone rounds from the pastry, never twist the cutter as the scones won't rise as well.

Chocolate Butterfly Cakes

These cakes have less butter icing than full-blown iced cupcakes, making them healthier and ideal for packed lunches!

PLAN AHEAD
Oven-cook recipe
Packed lunches and picnics
Double up
and freeze

Makes 12

175g butter	*For the icing*
175g sugar	75g butter
3 eggs, beaten	150–175g icing sugar
150g self-raising flour	1 tsp vanilla essence
30g cocoa	Few drops of water or milk
1 tbsp milk	

1   Preheat the oven to 200°C (gas mark 6).

2   In a bowl, cream the butter and sugar together until pale and fluffy. Then add the eggs, a little at a time, and continue to beat well.

3   Sift the flour and cocoa and gently fold into the mixture. When thoroughly mixed, add the milk.

4   Spoon the mixture into cupcake or muffin cases in a muffin or cupcake tray and bake for 12–18 minutes, depending on the size. The cakes should be firm and spring back when touched. Allow to cool.

5   Prepare the butter icing. In a bowl, beat the butter until soft. Gradually add the icing sugar and vanilla essence. Add a few drops of water or milk at a time until the icing is glossy, thick and lump-free.

6   Using a sharp knife, slice the top off each cake, plus a scoop of cake beneath. Cut these discs in half to create butterfly wings.

7 Fill the holes in the cakes with butter icing and place the wings on the top of the cakes, on their side, top side facing each other to create the wing shape. Sprinkle with icing sugar and you are ready to serve.

Apple and Date Muffins

These muffins are full of natural goodness and make a great addition to a packed lunch.

PLAN AHEAD
Oven-cook recipe
Packed lunches and picnics
Double up
and freeze

Makes 8

175g butter	2 tsp ground cinnamon
175g brown sugar	40g dates, chopped
3 eggs, beaten	75g dried apple rings, chopped
175g self-raising flour	

1 Preheat the oven to 190°C (gas mark 5).

2 In a bowl, cream the butter and sugar together until pale and fluffy. Add the eggs a little at a time and continue to beat well.

3 Sift the flour and gently fold into the mixture. Then add the cinnamon, dates and dried apple and combine well.

4 Spoon the mixture into muffin or cupcake cases in a muffin or cupcake tray and bake for 15–18 minutes. .

5 Cool on a rack or enjoy warm with a dollop of crème fraîche. Freeze once cooled, if freezing.

Mum's Lemon Curd Cupcakes

This is one of my mum's favourite recipes. The cupcakes are
ideal for packed lunches, but beware, they might not last that
long – they are yummy eaten when warm!

PLAN AHEAD
Oven-cook recipe
Packed lunches and picnics
Double up
and freeze

Makes 8–12

175g butter

150g sugar

3 large eggs, beaten

175g self-raising flour

1 tsp baking powder

125g sultanas

2 tbsp lemon curd

1 lemon for topping

100g sugar for topping

1   Preheat the oven to 190°C (gas mark 5).

2   Cream the butter and sugar together in a bowl until pale and fluffy.
    Then add the eggs a little at a time and continue to beat well.

3   Sift the flour and baking powder and gently fold into the mixture.
    When thoroughly mixed, gently fold in the sultanas and lemon curd.
    Don't overfold as you want the lemon curd to be more like a ripple
    effect.

4   Spoon the mixture into cupcake or muffin cases in a muffin or cup-
    cake tray and bake for 12–18 minutes depending on size. The cakes
    should be firm and spring back when touched.

5   Prepare the icing. Juice and zest 1 lemon. Mix the zest and juice
    together. Pour a little over each hot cake when you take them out
    of the oven and finish with a sprinkling of sugar.

─────────────────────── **Top Tip** ───────────────────────

*If you prefer a white icing look on the cakes instead of a drizzle,
mix a little lemon juice with icing sugar to make a thick icing.
Alternatively, freeze without the icing.*

Blueberry Muffins

These are so much nicer than the shop-bought variety. They freeze
well: take one out of the freezer to defrost in your lunch box by
lunchtime.

PLAN AHEAD
Oven-cook recipe
Packed lunches and picnics
Double up
and freeze

Makes 8–12

2 eggs, beaten	1 tsp vanilla extract
175g golden sugar	300g self-raising flour
250ml natural yoghurt	175g blueberries

1 Preheat the oven to 190°C (gas mark 5).

2 Beat the eggs and sugar together in a bowl until fluffy. Add the
   yoghurt and vanilla extract and beat again.

3 Sift the flour into the mixture and carefully fold in. When thoroughly
   mixed, add the blueberries.

4 Spoon the mixture into muffin or cupcake cases in a muffin or cupcake tray and bake for 15 minutes. Leave to cool before freezing, or
   store in an airtight container.

Upside-down Blackberry and Apple Cake

This makes an impressive display when you have friends around!

PLAN AHEAD

Oven-cook recipe
Packed lunches and picnics
Double up
and freeze

Serves 6–8

2–3 cooking apples, sliced

150g blackberries

175g sugar, plus 1 tbsp

175g butter, plus extra for greasing

3 eggs

175g self-raising flour, sifted

1 tsp vanilla extract

A sprinkling of icing sugar to decorate

1 Preheat the oven to 190°C (gas mark 5) and generously grease a 22 cm spring-form round cake tin with butter.

2 Place the apple slices, blackberries and 1 tablespoon of sugar in the base of your cake tin. I like to create a nice pattern on the base but you can be random – it all tastes the same!

3 Beat the butter and sugar in a bowl until light and fluffy. Add the eggs a little at a time, then add the sifted flour. Once mixed, add the vanilla extract. Combine well.

4 Pour the cake mixture over the apple and blackberries. Smooth the surface gently with a palette knife or spatula.

5 Place in the oven and bake for 30–40 minutes, until the cake is cooked, firm and springs back to shape when touched.

6 When ready to serve, place an upturned plate on the top of the cake tin. Flip over so the cake tin is upside down on top of the plate, and allow the cake to drop down onto the plate. If using a spring cake tin, undo this to release the cake.

7 Dust with sifted icing sugar to decorate before serving hot or cold.

Orange Loaf Cake

Another family favourite stolen from my mum's scrapbook of recipes! It is basically an orange drizzle cake, but you could also try lime instead of orange, or – for a really zingy drizzle – a combination of lime and lemon.

PLAN AHEAD
Oven-cook recipe
Packed lunches and picnics
Double up
and freeze

Serves 8–10

150g butter, plus extra for greasing

150g sugar

2 eggs

150g self-raising flour

2 tbsp milk

1 tsp orange essence

Zest and juice of one orange

3 tbsp icing sugar

Candied orange peel, to decorate (optional)

1   Preheat the oven to 180°C (gas mark 4) and grease a 454g loaf tin.

2   Beat the butter and sugar together in a bowl until creamy. Add the eggs, beat again and then add the flour, milk, orange essence and zest.

3   Pour the mixture into the tin and bake for 20–30 minutes, until firm and cooked. Turn out onto a cooling rack.

4   Mix the orange juice and icing sugar together in a cup and pour this over the cooled cake. Decorate with a few slices of candied orange peel.

Cooking Tip

Test that your cake is cooked properly by inserting a clean skewer into the centre. If the skewer is clean when you pull it out, your cake is cooked. If some cake clings to the skewer, pop the cake back into the oven for a few minutes, then check again.

Viennese Whirls

This is a recipe where you really do need to use a good-quality butter, as margarine does not give the same taste or result.

PLAN AHEAD
Oven-cook recipe
Packed lunches and picnics
Double up
and freeze

Makes 18–22 biscuits

200g unsalted butter, plus extra
  for greasing

50g icing sugar

½ tsp vanilla paste

150g plain flour, sifted

50g cornflour, sifted

1   Preheat the oven to 190°C (gas mark 5) and grease a baking tray.

2   Beat the butter, icing sugar and vanilla paste together in a bowl until light and fluffy.

3   Gradually add the sifted flour and cornflour until you have a firm but squeezable paste.

4   Spoon the paste into a piping bag and, holding this firmly, pipe swirly biscuits approximately 6–7cm in diameter onto the baking tray. If you don't have a piping bag, carefully spoon dollops of the mixture onto the tray, but these will not be as neat when they cook.

5   Place in the oven and bake for 10–15 minutes, until golden. Cool on a rack, then store in an airtight container for up to one week.

Extra Recipes

This is a great recipe to use for topping mince pies or jam tarts instead of a traditional pastry top. Simply pipe directly onto the pie before you bake.

Coconut and Fruit Flapjack

You can vary this recipe by using chopped apricots, dates or cranberries for a different flavour or to use up oddments of dried fruit that are lurking in your cupboard. For a decadent touch, coat or dip the slices in dark chocolate.

PLAN AHEAD
Oven-cook recipe
Packed lunches and picnics
Double up
and freeze

Makes 8 pieces

175g butter, plus extra for greasing	250g oats
25g golden syrup	50g desiccated coconut
125g brown sugar	50g raisins

1 Preheat the oven to 180°C (gas mark 4) and grease a baking tin.

2 Put the butter and syrup into a bowl and place in the microwave, heating gently for 30 seconds at a time (full power). Stir the mixture before heating again; it should only take about a minute. Alternatively melt the butter and syrup in a heavy base saucepan and continue to use this saucepan as your mixing bowl to save on washing up.

3 Add all the remaining ingredients to the melted butter and syrup and stir well.

4 Tip the flapjack mixture into your prepared tin and press down firmly. Place in the oven and bake for 10–15 minutes.

5 Cut the flapjacks into slices while in the tin, then allow to cool before removing them. Alternatively, store in an airtight container, or freeze.

Banana and Chocolate Loaf Cake

I am not a fan of plain banana cakes but found that if I added cocoa I enjoyed it more – probably because I'm a bit of a chocolate addict! This is a great recipe to use up those brown bananas lurking in your fruit bowl. You can also use defrosted bananas.

PLAN AHEAD
Oven-cook recipe
Packed lunches and picnics
Double up
and freeze

Serves 8

125g sugar

125g butter, plus extra for greasing

2 tbsp honey

1 tsp vanilla essence

2 eggs, beaten

1 ripe mashed banana

150g self-raising flour, sifted

4 tbsp cocoa, sifted

Melted chocolate or vanilla icing (page 238), to decorate (optional)

1   Preheat the oven to 190°C (gas mark 5) and grease or line a loaf tin.

2   Using an electric mixer, beat the sugar and butter together in a bowl until light and fluffy. Add the honey, vanilla essence and beaten eggs; mix again.

3   Add the banana, before adding the sifted flour and cocoa. Combine well. Pour the mixture into the tin and bake for 30 minutes, or until skewer comes out clean when pushed into the centre of the cake.

4   Remove from the oven and leave to cool slightly before turning out onto a cooling rack. Continue to decorate as below, or you can now freeze to use later.

5   Enjoy plain or decorate with melted chocolate or vanilla buttercream.

Date and Walnut Slice

This is a delicious and healthy alternative to a cake. For added naughtiness you could add a handful of plain chocolate chips to the mixture.

PLAN AHEAD
Oven-cook recipe
Packed lunches and picnics
Double up
and freeze

Makes 8 slices

50g butter	1 egg, beaten
75g oats	2 tbsp natural yoghurt
30g brown sugar, plus extra for sprinkling	1 tsp vanilla essence
30g plain flour	50g self-raising flour
75g sugar	100g chopped dates
	50g chopped walnuts

1   Heat the butter in the microwave (full power for 850 watt microwave) for 20–30 seconds (making sure it doesn't burn). Alternatively, melt the butter in a heavy base saucepan and continue to use this saucepan as your mixing bowl to save on washing up. Once the butter has melted, stir in the oats, brown sugar and plain flour.

2   Press the mixture into a lined 30cm x 20cm rectangular baking tray to form the base of the slices.

3   Preheat the oven to 180°C (gas mark 4). While the oven warms up, beat the sugar and egg together in a bowl. Once light and fluffy, add the yoghurt and vanilla essence.

4   Add the self-raising flour, dates and most of the walnuts, retaining a few to use on the top of the slices. Pour the mixture on top of the base and spread with a palette knife to cover evenly.

5   Sprinkle with the remaining walnuts and a little brown sugar before baking for 20 minutes. Leave to cool for 5–10 minutes before slicing. Store in an airtight container or freeze.

Easter Muffins

Here is a lovely fruit and spice muffin, which – despite the name – can be enjoyed at any time of the year!

PLAN AHEAD

Oven-cook recipe
Packed lunches and picnics
Double up
and freeze

Makes 6–8

125g self-raising flour, sifted

50g sugar

75g dried fruit (currants, sultanas, raisins)

2–3 tsp ground cinnamon

½ tsp nutmeg

275ml milk

1 egg, beaten

4 tbsp olive oil

1   Preheat the oven to 180°C (gas mark 4).

2   In a mixing bowl, combine the sifted flour and the other dry ingredients.

3   Place the milk in a jug and beat in the egg and olive oil. Combine well before pouring this onto the dried ingredients. Mix thoroughly.

4   Once combined, spoon the mixture into muffin tins, either greased or lined with paper muffin cases.

5   Place in the oven and bake for 20–25 minutes – the muffins should spring back into shape when pressed.

6   Cool on a wire rack before freezing or storing in an airtight container.

Rhubarb Flapjack Bars

These are seriously yummy and quite filling so don't cut them into large slices!

PLAN AHEAD

Oven-cook recipe
Packed lunches and picnics
Double up
and freeze

Makes 8–12 slices

400g rhubarb, (trimmed)	200g brown sugar
2 tbsp sugar	300g oats
1 tbsp water	125g plain flour
300g butter, plus extra for greasing	1–2 tsp ground cinnamon
3 tbsp golden syrup	50g chopped nuts

1 Preheat the oven to 180°C (gas mark 4) and grease or line a 23cm baking tin.

2 Chop the rhubarb into chunks and place in a pan. Add the sugar and water. Cook gently on a medium heat until soft, stirring occasionally.

3 Meanwhile, place the butter and golden syrup in an ovenproof dish to melt in the microwave (full power at 850 watt microwave) or over a pan of just-simmering water. Don't allow it to burn! Stir until combined.

4 Put the remaining dry ingredients in a bowl and, when the butter and syrup mixture has melted, pour it over the dried mixture and combine.

5 Press half the mixture into the baking tray, pressing down firmly. Spread the cooked rhubarb over the base.

6 Add the remaining oat mixture to form a top and press down well. Place in the oven and bake for 20 minutes until golden.

7 Leave to cool before removing from the tin and cutting into slices.

8 Store for 3–4 days in an airtight contaianer or freeze for up to one month.

Carrot Cake Muffins with Vanilla Icing

Another delicious treat for the lunchbox!

PLAN AHEAD
Oven-cook recipe
Packed lunches and picnics
Double up
and freeze

Makes 8–12

For the cakes

175g butter

175g brown sugar

3 eggs, beaten

175g self-raising flour

2 tsp cinnamon powder

1 tsp ground coriander

2 carrots, grated

50g desiccated coconut

For the vanilla icing

50g butter

100g cream cheese

200–275g icing sugar

1 tsp vanilla essence or paste

Fondant icing carrots to decorate
  (optional)

1   Preheat the oven to 190°C (gas mark 5).

2   Cream the butter and sugar together in a bowl until pale and fluffy.
    Then add the eggs a little at a time and continue to beat well.

3   Sift the flour and gently fold into the mixture. When thoroughly
    mixed, add the cinnamon, coriander, grated carrot and coconut;
    combine well.

4   Spoon the mixture into muffin or cupcake cases in a muffin or cup-
    cake tray and bake for 15–20 minutes. Allow to cool on a rack.

5   Once cooled, you can freeze or you can begin to ice the cakes. To
    make the icing, beat the butter and cream cheese together in a bowl
    until soft. Gradually add the icing sugar and vanilla essence or paste
    and beat until the icing is glossy, thick and lump-free.

6   Place the icing in an icing bag and fold down the ends to secure.
    Start on the outside of the cooled cakes and spiral inwards to cover

the whole of the cake top, gently overlapping to avoid gaps. Decorate with fondant icing carrots, if liked.

Chocolate and Date Fingers

This is a lovely chocolatey flapjack style snack and it is very addictive. All you need is a lovely cup of tea, a good book and a comfy sofa – life cannot get any better!

PLAN AHEAD
Oven-cook recipe
Packed lunches and picnics
Double up
and freeze

Makes 8–10 pieces

60g plain cooking chocolate	1 tbsp golden syrup
185g butter	125g dates, roughly chopped
60g brown sugar	250g oats

1   Preheat the oven to 180°C (gas mark 4) and grease a baking tin or ovenproof dish.

2   In a saucepan, melt the chocolate, butter, sugar and syrup on a low to medium heat, making sure this does not burn. Stir continuously.

3   Add the chopped dates and the oats and mix well.

4   Tip into your prepared tin and press down gently.

5   Place in the oven and cook for 20 minutes.

6   Leave to cool in the tin before cutting into fingers. Alternatively, store in an airtight container, or freeze

Cappuccino Cupcakes

I recently found some chocolates in the shape of coffee beans, which look amazing on top.

PLAN AHEAD
Oven-cook recipe
Packed lunches and picnics
Double up
and freeze

Makes 8–12

For the cakes	For the icing
175g butter	50g butter
175g sugar	100g cream cheese
3 eggs, beaten	200–275g icing sugar
175g self-raising flour	1 tsp vanilla essence or paste
2–4 tsp coffee essence, depending on desired strength	sprinkling of cocoa, to decorate

1 Preheat the oven to 190°C (gas mark 5).

2 Cream the butter and sugar together in a bowl until pale and fluffy. Then add the eggs a little at a time and continue to beat well.

3 Sift the flour and gently fold into the mixture. When thoroughly mixed, add the coffee essence to taste and combine.

4 Spoon the mixture into muffin or cupcake cases in a muffin or cupcake tray and bake for 15 minutes. The cakes should be firm and spring back when touched. Allow to cool on a rack. Once cool, the cakes can be frozen.

5 Prepare the icing. Beat the butter and cream cheese together in a bowl until soft. Gradually add the icing sugar and vanilla essence or paste and beat until the icing is glossy, thick and lump-free.

6 Place the icing in an icing bag and fold down the ends to secure. Start in the centre of each cake and spiral outwards to cover the whole cake top, gently overlapping to avoid gaps. Finish with a sprinkling of cocoa to give a cappuccino effect.

Boiled Fruit Tea Loaf

Ideally, the fruit and the tea are left overnight so the fruit absorbs the liquid, resulting in a moist loaf that is delicious sliced and spread with a little butter.

PLAN AHEAD
Oven-cook recipe
Packed lunches and picnics
Double up
and freeze

Makes 8–10 slices

300g mixed dried fruit	2 tsp cinnamon
125g butter, plus extra for greasing	1 tsp allspice
125g brown sugar	40g dried apple rings,
220ml stewed tea	225g self-raising flour

1 Place the dried fruit, butter and brown sugar in a large pan. Add the tea.

2 Place the pan over a moderate heat, stirring gently, until the butter melts and the sugar has dissolved. Keep stirring as you don't want this to stick or burn. Once melted, add the spices. Boil for one minute then remove from the heat.

3 Using sharp scissors, snip the apple rings into pieces and drop into the pan. Stir well and leave until cold, or overnight if you prefer.

4 Once cooled, sift in the flour and stir well until thoroughly combined. Preheat the oven to 160°C (gas mark 3).

5 Thoroughly grease or line your loaf tin and pour in the mixture.

6 Bake for 40–50 minutes, or until a skewer inserted into the centre of the cake comes out clean.

7 Leave to cool in the cake tin before turning out onto a cooling rack.

Lemon Cream Sponge

For an extra lemon tang, add a little lemon essence, but buy a
good-quality one or it can taste artificial.

PLAN AHEAD
Oven-cook recipe
Packed lunches and picnics
Double up
and freeze

Serves 8

For the sponge	For the icing
175g butter, plus extra for greasing	50g butter
175g sugar	100g cream cheese
3 eggs, beaten	300g icing sugar
200g self-raising flour	2–3 tbsp lemon curd
Zest and juice of 2–3 lemons	Lemon slices, to decorate

1   Preheat the oven to 190°C (gas mark 5).

2   Cream the butter and sugar together in a bowl until pale and fluffy.
    Then add the eggs a little at a time and continue to beat well.

3   Sift the flour and gently fold into the mixture. When thoroughly
    mixed, add the zest and juice of the lemons and combine.

4   Place the mixture in two greased sponge tins and bake for 20 min-
    utes until firm to the touch and the cakes have pulled away slightly
    from the edges of the tins.

5   While the cakes are cooling, prepare the butter icing. Alternatively,
    you can freeze the cakes now. Beat the butter and cream cheese
    together in a bowl until soft. Gradually add the icing sugar and beat
    until the icing is glossy, thick and lump-free.

6   Spread the butter icing on one of the sponges and lemon curd on
    the other then sandwich together. This is less messy than trying to
    spread butter icing on top of lemon curd. If you prefer, you can add
    icing to the top or around the sides, or even all over the cake. Finish
    with a couple of slices of lemon to decorate.

PLANNING AHEAD

We all tend to eat the same foods week after week for most of the time, so really you only need a few weeks' worth of menu plans to get you going. The secret to the success of menu planning is your ability to plan ahead, thus saving you time and money. If you take a few minutes to plan ahead, you will find that you cut down on waste dramatically. I urge you to use your freezer – if you don't have a freezer, invest in one as you will find it invaluable. In my kitchen, I have an undercounter freezer where I keep everyday items. I also have a small chest freezer in my garage for bulk storage.

Mastering the art of planning

In this section I am giving you the freedom to choose certain elements. On pages 256–63 I have provided a Quick Reference Guide to help you find the recipes you need quickly and easily. These pages are all broken down into the way the food is cooked (Slow cooker, Hob and Grill, Oven-cook) and also show those recipes that can be frozen. I have added some ideas for packed lunches. These items are not exclusively for packed lunches – they can, of course, form part of a meal or everyday cakes and snacks but they are provided to give you some ideas. In the menu planner, if I suggest a meal for the oven, I will also suggest that you choose something else to cook to fill the oven space – this is where the packed lunch section can be worthwhile.

Double up and freeze

I cannot emphasise this enough – double up and freezing has got to be part of your everyday cooking – it will revolutionise your time in the kitchen, enabling you to have more free time, less waste and home-cooked meals at your convenience. It really takes little time to double up a recipe and make two or three meals instead of one. Remember to label everything before you put it in the freezer. Refer back to the Making the Most of Your Freezer section (pages 7–17) for more information.

Have a Batch Cooking Day

This is a really simple concept. Put aside a few hours a week to have a batch cooking session. This will fill your freezer with homemade ready meals, leaving you more time to spend with your family after a busy day. To do this, decide on your main ingredient and plan your recipes. If there are favourite foods your family likes week after week, there is nothing wrong with just doing one recipe and making three or four meals. Remember the golden rule, label and date everything as you don't want to end up with meals that stay in the freezer for months. Below is an example.

Mince

Go to the mince chapter (pages 123–134) and you will see a variety of family dishes that you can make with mince. You might also want to add a few of your own. List what you are going to make and the ingredients you need. Mince is an easy one as most dishes follow the same opening principles of onion, garlic and mince before adding your additional ingredients. I usually do this first step in a very large stock pot and then decide what I am going to make from there.

Make sure you have the containers ready with the labels and everything you need.

Within an hour or two you will have several meals prepared.

You can do the same for chicken dishes and work through the same principles as above. Chicken and mince are my favourites – you will also find that most supermarkets do great deals on buying three chicken or mince combinations so you can save additional cash. Speak to your butcher as he/she can often sell you larger quantities for a better price.

Menu Planner

On the pages that follow you will find a suggested menu plan. Follow this to the letter if you like, but it is good if you can make your own plan to suit your family's requirements. Most families tend to stick to the same meals and just rotate them so you will find it is far easier to put this together than you might think. Try to follow a pattern to make the most of any leftovers as well as your time and remember the golden rules of doubling up and freezing, allowing you to get ahead. I keep saying the same thing but really, it takes no more time to double up and saves you significant time and money in the long term.

DAY	MEAL	USE YOUR OVEN
Sunday	Roast chicken, roast potatoes, vegetables and gravy	Remember your oven is on, so make the most of it by filling it! Have a look at the index of oven-cook recipes and choose something to suit.
Monday – Leftover day. Slow cook or hob recipe	Simple Chicken Curry (or whatever dish you made with yesterday's leftover chicken)	This can be made in the slow cooker or you can follow the same recipe and cook on the hob.
Tuesday – Double up.	Spaghetti Bolognaise	
Wednesday	Salmon and Herb Butter Parcels with new potatoes and green vegetables	Remember your oven is on, so make the most of it by filling it Have a look at the index of oven-cook recipes and choose something to suit.
Thursday – Slow cooker day.	Irish Lamb Stew	This recipe is made in the slow cooker, so remember you can prepare it the night before or in the morning before you start your day.
Friday – Double up	Creamy Fish Pie and peas	

TOP TIP	USE YOUR LEFTOVERS
Buy a larger chicken than you need for one meal and this can be used to make one or two more meals.	**Roast Chicken** can be turned into: Simple Chicken Curry; chicken casseroles; Cheat's Left-over Chicken Pie; Tandoori Chicken; Chicken Tikka; Chicken and Cumin Soup. **Vegetables** can be turned into: Bubble and Squeak Patties; Vegetable Frittata; Vegetable Mornay.
Add a tin of chickpeas to the curry and make it stretch further; this also adds protein and aids digestion.	
Double up this recipe – you can use this as a base for a lasagne or even a chilli.	
You can prepare the parcels in the morning, ready for you to pop into the oven when you get home.	Double up your new potatoes – you can use them in tomorrow's stew. Slice Slice them to put on the top to create a Lamb Hotpot or just serve them quartered in the stew itself.
Double up the recipe and pop one in the freezer.	

DAY	MEAL	USE YOUR OVEN
Saturday – Slow cooker day.	Moroccan-style Vegetable Tagine with Quinoa	
Sunday	Roast beef, roast potatoes, Yorkshire pudding, vegetables and gravy	Remember, your oven is on, so make the most of it by filling it! Have a look at the index of oven-cook recipes and choose something to suit.
Monday – Leftover day.	Beef Stroganoff with rice, or whatever dish you choose to make with your leftover beef.	
Tuesday – Double up.	Spinach and Ricotta Lasagne with salad	Remember, your oven is on, so make the most of it by filling it! Have a look at the index of oven-cook recipes and choose something to suit.
Wednesday	Spicy Moroccan-style Lamb Cutlets, green vegetables and mash	
Thursday – Easy day.	Toad in the Hole, new potatoes and green vegetables.	Remember, your oven is on, so make the most of it by filling it! Have a look at the index of oven-cook recipes and choose something to suit.

TOP TIP	USE YOUR LEFTOVERS
This is a slow cooker recipe, so you can prepare it before you go out for the day or even the night before.	
Buy a larger joint of beef so you can turn this into additional meals. Cook some sausages in the oven and double up your Yorkshire pudding recipe, then pour the extra batter over your baked sausages and allow to cool. Freeze once cool as already-made Toad in the Hole for another occasion.	Leftover beef can be used to fill sandwiches or in a range of meals such as: Beef Stroganoff; Beef stir-fry; Cornish pasties; or Healthy Beef Curry. You can also mince up the leftover beef to create any of the recipes from the Mince chapter.
You can double up this recipe to add one to the freezer, or just double up the spinach and ricotta mixture and add to a pastry case. Or line a tin with filo pastry to make a spinach and ricotta filo pie.	
Remove the Toad in the Hole from the freezer (made on Sunday, see above) ready for tomorrow's dinner.	

DAY	MEAL	USE YOUR OVEN
Friday – Double up.	Salmon, Sweet Potato and Chilli Fish Cakes, chips and peas	
Saturday – Double up.	Lasagne with salad and garlic bread	Remember, your oven is on so make the most of it by filling it
Sunday	Roast chicken, roast potatoes, vegetables and gravy	Remember, your oven is on, so make the most of it by filling it! Have a look at the index of oven-cook recipes and choose something to suit.
Monday – Leftover day.	Cheat's Leftover Chicken Pie with mash and green vegetables	Remember, your oven is on, so make the most of it by filling it! Have a look at the index of oven-cook recipes and choose something to suit.

TOP TIP	USE YOUR LEFTOVERS
Double up the recipe and freeze a batch.	
Double up the recipe and freeze another lasagne. Alternatively, double up the mince and you will have a sauce to freeze, ready for Spaghetti Bolognaise. You can also double up the cheese sauce and use it to make a cauliflower cheese, Vegetable Mornay or even a cheesy fish pie. When making garlic bread, you can double up and freeze one for another time, or double up the garlic butter and freeze it in rounds or a log to use in a baked fish dish.	
Buy a larger chicken than you need for one meal and you can use the leftovers to make one or two more meals.	Roast chicken can be turned into: Simple Chicken Curry; Chicken Casseroles; Cheat's Leftover Chicken Pie; Tandoori Chicken; Chicken Tikka; Chicken and Cumin Soup. Vegetables can be turned into: Bubble and Squeak Patties; Vegetable Frittata; Vegetable Mornay.
Take the mince from the freezer (doubled up from making lasagne last week) and allow it to defrost in the fridge, ready to use as Spaghetti Bolognaise tomorrow.	If you are making pastry for this meal, why not create some other pastry dishes and freeze them? I suggest Quiche Lorraine, as it can be used for a meal this week.

DAY	MEAL	USE YOUR OVEN
Tuesday – Easy day.	Spaghetti Bolognaise	
Wednesday – Easy day.	Quiche Lorraine with new potatoes and salad	
Thursday – Slow cooker day.	Beef Bourguignon	
Friday – Easy day.	Fish pie with peas	
Saturday	Bacon, Leek and Macaroni Cheese Bake	Remember, your oven is on, so make the most of it by filling it! Have a look at the index of oven-cook recipes and choose something to suit.
Sunday	Roast lamb, roast potatoes	Remember, your oven is on, so make the most of it by filling it! Have a look at the index of oven-cook recipes and choose something to suit.

TOP TIP	USE YOUR LEFTOVERS
Remove the Quiche Lorraine from the freezer and leave to defrost in the fridge.	
This is a slow cooker recipe, so you can prepare it the night before or in the morning before you start your day. Remove the fish pie you made two weeks ago from the freezer.	
Double up the size of the joint to make more dishes, such as Lamb and Green Lentil Curry (for tomorrow night's dinner) or Tunisian Lamb. You can also use the lamb to make pasties, fill sandwiches or wraps, or mince it to make a Shepherd's Pie.	

DAY	MEAL	USE YOUR OVEN
Monday – Slow cooker day.	Lamb and Green Lentil Curry	This recipe can also be made on the hob.
Tuesday – Quick hob recipe	Squash Soup with Spiced Yoghurt	
Wednesday – Easy day.	Spinach and Ricotta Lasagne	Remember, your oven is on, so make the most of it by filling it. Have a look at the index of oven-cook recipes and choose something to suit.
Thursday – Slow cooker day.	Hearty Chicken Casserole	
Friday – Easy day.	Salmon, Sweet Potato and Chilli Fish Cakes	
Saturday – Grill recipe	Sticky Chicken Drumsticks with rice and salad	

TOP TIP	USE YOUR LEFTOVERS
This recipe is made in the slow cooker, so remember you can prepare it the night before or in the morning, before you start your day	This recipe uses up yesterday's leftover lamb from the joint.
Remove the Spinach and Ricotta Lasagne (or pie) made two weeks ago from the freezer, ready for tomorrow's dinner.	
This recipe is made in the slow cooker, so remember, you can prepare it the night before or in the morning before you start your day. You can also double up this recipe for another occasion.	
Use the fish cakes you made and froze two weeks ago.	

Quick Reference Guide

Slow Cook Recipes

Light Meals and Snacks
- Chicken, Cumin and Harissa Soup
- Chunky Winter Vegetable and Lentil Hotpot
- Chunky Winter Vegetable and Lentil Soup
- Minestrone Soup
- Red Tomato, Pepper and Sweet Potato Soup

Poultry
- Cajun Chicken Casserole
- Cheat's Chicken Tikka
- Cheat's Chicken and Vegetable Curry
- Chicken Vindaloo
- Coq au Vin
- Hearty Chicken Casserole
- Moroccan-style Chicken and Vegetable Tagine
- Simple Chicken Curry

Meat
- Beef and Ale Stew with Herb Dumplings
- Beef Bourguignon
- Ham Hock
- Healthy Beef Curry
- Irish Lamb Stew
- Lamb and Green Lentil Curry
- Lamb Shanks
- Spicy Beef and Bean Casserole
- Tunisian Lamb
- Wholesome Lamb and Vegetable Casserole

Fish
- Halibut, Chilli and Vegetable Casserole
- Italian Baked Cod
- Seafood Aljotta

Vegetarian
- Moroccan-style Vegetable Tagine with Quinoa
- Vegetable Korma

Oven-cook Recipes

Light Meals and Snacks
- Cheese and Potato Puffs
- Cheese and Spring Onion Quiche
- Cheese and Vegetable Pasties
- Cheese Scones
- Corned Beef and Potato Tart
- Goats' cheese and Red Onion Tarts
- Goats' Cheese, Pesto and Cherry Tomato Tart
- Herby Sausage Rolls
- Homemade Pizza
- Homemade Potato Wedges
- Hot, Hot, Hot Sausage Rolls
- Mediterranean-style Tortilla
- Mozzarella and Cherry Tomato Tarts
- Pizza Puffs
- Puffed Sausage Rolls
- Quiche Lorraine
- Roasted Vegetables and Feta Tart
- Sausage and Herb En Croute
- Sausage in a Blanket
- Spinach and Feta Filo Pie
- Sun-dried Tomato and Goats Cheese Frittata
- Tofu and Spinach Quiche
- Traditional Cornish Pasties
- Tuna and Sweetcorn Puff Tarts

Poultry
- Cheat's Leftover Chicken Pie
- Homemade Chicken Nuggets
- Roasted Herby Vegetables and Chicken Breasts
- Roasted Squash One-Pot Chicken
- Spicy Chicken Wings
- Tandoori Chicken

Meat
- Bacon, Leek and Macaroni Cheese Bake
- Corned Beef Loaf
- Ham and Leek Cheesy Bake
- Roasted Cherry Tomato, Pancetta and Ricotta Pasta
- Stuffed Loin of Pork
- Toad in the Hole

Mince
- Lasagne
- Moussaka
- Shepherd's and Cottage Pie

Fish
- Baked Herbie Salmon
- Cheesy Pollock Layer
- Cod and Cheese Gratin
- Creamy Baked Haddock
- Creamy Fish Pie

- Haddock, Egg and Gruyère Bake
- Haddock Florentine
- One-pot Roasted Fish, Fennel and Red Onion
- Salmon, Garlic and White Wine Parcels
- Salmon and Herb Butter Parcels
- Salmon with a Honey and Mustard Crust
- Salmon and Prawn Puff Pie
- Salmon, Ricotta and Cheese Cannelloni
- Smoked Mackerel and Leek Pie
- Thai Fish Bakes
- Tomato and Tuna Gratin

Vegetarian
- Homemade Potato Weges
- Leek and Cheese Sausages
- Mushroom and Cashew Nut Roast
- Spicy Bean and Tomato Stuffed Butternut Squash
- Spinach and Ricotta Lasagne
- Vegetable and Bean Crumble
- Vegetable Mornay Bake

Desserts
- Apple and Blackberry Pie
- Apple and Blackcurrant Crumble
- Apple and Blueberry Crumble
- Apple and Cinnamon Cobbler
- Apple and Date Bread and Butter Pudding
- Apple, Sultana and Cinnamon Pie
- Baked Bananas with Dark Chocolate Sauce
- Baked Cinnamon Apples
- Blackberry and Apple Crumble
- Cheat's Ginger and Apple Layer
- Chocolate, Pear and Hazelnut Betty
- Chocolate Saucy Pudding
- Gooseberry and Elderflower Crumble
- Gooseberry Betty
- Lemon Saucy Pudding
- Pear and Dark Chocolate Granola Layer
- Pineapple Upside-down Cake
- Queen of Puddings
- Rhubarb Crumble
- Rhubarb and Ginger Crumble
- Simple Cheating Eccles Cakes
- Spiced Apple Crumble
- Strawberry and Rhubarb Crumble
- Summer Fruit Crumble

Treats
- Apple and Date Muffins
- Banana and Chocolate Loaf Cake
- Blueberry Muffins
- Blueberry Scones
- Boiled Fruit Tea Loaf
- Cappuccino Cupcakes

- Carrot Cake Muffins with Vanilla Icing
- Chocolate and Date Fingers
- Chocolate Butterfly Cakes
-

- Chocolate Chip Cupcakes with Vanilla Icing
- Coconut and Fruit Flapjack
- Date and Walnut Slice
- Death by Chocolate Cake
- Easter Muffins
- Fruit Scones
- Lemon Cream Sponge
- Mum's Lemon Curd Cupcakes
- Orange Loaf Cake
- Rhubarb Flapjack Bars
- Upside-down Blackberry and Apple Cake
- Viennese Whirls

Hob and Grill Recipes

Light Meals and Snacks
- Bubble and Squeak Patties
- Carrot and Courgette Soup
- Pea and Ham Soup
- Red Pepper and Tomato Soup with Pesto Swirl
- Squash Soup with Spiced Yoghurt
- Tomato, Lentil and Carrot Soup

Poultry
- Chicken and Mushroom Casserole
- Chicken, Bacon and Bean Casserole
- Chicken Burgers

- Chicken Chow Mien
- Chicken, Pepper and Tomato Pasta
- Spring Chicken Casserole
- Sticky Chicken Drumsticks

Meat
- Bacon and Mushroom Pasta
- Beef Stroganoff
- Quick and Easy Garlic, Mushroom and Ham Tagliatelle
- Sausage Casserole
- Spicy Moroccan-style Lamb Cutlets
- Sweet and Sour Pork

Mince

- Basic Mince Recipe
- Beef and Bacon Burgers
- Beefburgers
- Spicy Meatballs in Rich Tomato Sauce

Fish

- Fishburgers
- Prawn and Asparagus Pasta
- Salmon, Sweet Potato and Chilli Fish Cakes
- Smoked Haddock with Leek and Parsley Sauce
- Tomato, Prawn and Fish Stew

Vegetarian

- Leek and Cheese Sausages
- Lentil Dahl
- Mushroom and Goats' Cheese Bakes
- Mushroom Risotto
- Ratatouille
- Spicy Spinach and Potato
- Thai Bean Cakes
- Tofu and Chickpea Burgers
- Tuscan Tomato and Bean
- Vegetable Curry

Desserts

- Butterscotch Sauce
- Fruit Compôte
- Homemade Custard
- No-messing Rice Pudding
- Summer Pudding

Double Up and Freeze Recipes

Light Meals and Snacks

- Bubble and Squeak Patties
- Carrot and Courgette Soup
- Cheese and Potato Puffs
- Cheese and Spring Onion Quiche
- Cheese and Vegetable Pasties
- Cheese Scones
- Chicken, Cumin and Harissa Soup
- Chunky Winter Vegetable and Lentil Hotpot
- Chunky Winter Vegetable and Lentil Soup
- Corned Beef and Potato Tart
- Goats' Cheese and Red Onion Tarts
- Goats' Cheese, Pesto and Cherry Tomato Tart
- Herby Sausage Rolls
- Homemade Pizza
- Hot, Hot, Hot Sausage Rolls
- Minestrone Soup
- Pea and Ham Soup
- Puffed Sausage Rolls

- Quiche Lorraine
- Red Pepper and Tomato Soup with Pesto Swirl
- Red Tomato, Pepper and Sweet Potato Soup
- Sausage and Herb En Croute
- Sausage in a Blanket
- Spinach and Feta Filo Pie
- Squash Soup with Spiced Yoghurt
- Tofu and Spinach Quiche
- Tomato, Lentil and Carrot Soup
- Traditional Cornish Pasties

Poultry

- Cajun Chicken Casserole
- Cheat's Chicken Tikka
- Cheat's Chicken and Vegetable Curry
- Cheat's Leftover Chicken Pie
- Chicken and Mushroom Casserole
- Chicken Burgers
- Chicken, Bacon and Bean Casserole
- Chicken Vindaloo
- Coq au Vin

Mince

- Basic Mince Recipe
- Beef and Bacon Burgers
- Beefburgers
- Lasagne
- Moussaka
- Shepherd's and Cottage Pie
- Spicy Meatballs in Rich Tomato Sauce

Fish

- Cod and Cheese Gratin
- Creamy Fish Pie
- Fishburgers
- Halibut, Chilli and Vegetable Casserole
- Salmon and Prawn Puff Pie
- Salmon, Ricotta and Cheese Cannelloni
- Salmon, Sweet Potato and Chilli Fish Cakes
- Seafood Aljotta
- Smoked Mackerel and Leek Pie
- Thai Fish Bakes

Vegetarian

- Leek and Cheese Sausages
- Lentil Dahl
- Moroccan-style Vegetable Tagine with Quinoa
- Mushroom and Cashew Nut Roast
- Ratatouille
- Spicy Spinach and Potato
- Spinach and Ricotta Lasagne
- Thai Bean Cakes
- Tofu and Chickpea Burgers
- Vegetable and Bean Crumble
- Vegetable Curry
- Vegetable Korma
- Vegetable Mornay Bake

Desserts

- Apple and Blackberry Pie
- Apple and Blackcurrant Crumble
- Apple and Blueberry Crumble
- Apple and Date Bread and Butter Pudding
- Apple and Cinnamon Cobbler
- Apple, Sultana and Cinnamon Pie
- Blackberry and Apple Crumble
- Chocolate, Pear and Hazelnut Betty
- Fruit Compôte
- Gooseberry and Elderflower Crumble
- Gooseberry Betty
- Homemade Custard
- No-messing Rice Pudding
- Oaty Crumble Mix
- Pineapple Upside-down Cake
- Rhubarb and Ginger Crumble
- Rhubarb Crumble
- Simple Cheating Eccles Cakes
- Spiced Apple Crumble
- Strawberry and Rhubarb Crumble
- Summer Fruit Crumble
- Summer Pudding

Treats

- Apple and Date Muffins
- Banana and Chocolate Loaf Cake
- Blueberry Muffins
- Blueberry Scones
- Boiled Fruit Tea Loaf
- Cappuccino Cupcakes
- Carrot Cake Muffins with Vanilla Icing
- Chocolate and Date Fingers
- Chocolate Butterfly Cakes
- Chocolate Chip Cupcakes with Vanilla Icing
- Coconut and Fruit Flapjack
- Date and Walnut Slice
- Death by Chocolate Cake
- Easter Muffins
- Fruit Scones
- Lemon Cream Sponge
- Mum's Lemon Curd Cupcakes
- Orange Loaf Cake
- Rhubarb Flapjack Bars
- Upside-down Blackberry and Apple Cake
- Viennese Whirls

Packed Lunch and Picnic Recipes

Light Meals and Snacks

- Bubble and Squeak Patties
- Cheese and Potato Puffs
- Cheese and Spring Onion Quiche
- Cheese and Vegetable Pasties
- Cheese Scones
- Corned Beef and Potato Tart
- Goats' Cheese and Red Onion Tarts
- Goats' Cheese, Pesto and Cherry Tomato Tart
- Herby Sausage Rolls
- Homemade Pizza
- Hot, Hot, Hot Sausage Rolls
- Mediterranean-style Tortilla
- Mozzarella and Cherry Tomato Tarts
- Pizza Puffs
- Puffed Sausage Rolls
- Quiche Lorraine
- Roasted Vegetables and Feta Tart
- Sausage and Herb En Croute
- Sausage in a Blanket
- Spinach and Feta Filo Pie
- Sun-dried Tomato and Goats' Cheese Frittata
- Tofu and Spinach Quiche
- Traditional Cornish Pasties
- Tuna and Sweetcorn Puff Tarts

Desserts

- Apple and Blackberry Pie
- Apple, Sultana and Cinnamon Pie
- Pineapple Upside-down Cake
- Simple Cheating Eccles Cakes

Treats

- Apple and Date Muffins
- Banana and Chocolate Loaf Cake
- Blueberry Muffins
- Blueberry Scones
- Boiled Fruit Tea Loaf
- Cappuccino Cupcakes
- Carrot Cake Muffins with Vanilla Icing
- Chocolate and Date Fingers
- Chocolate Butterfly Cakes
- Chocolate Chip Cupcakes with Vanilla Icing
- Coconut and Fruit Flapjack
- Date and Walnut Slice
- Death by Chocolate Cake
- Easter Muffins
- Fruit Scones
- Lemon Cream Sponge
- Mum's Lemon Curd Cupcakes
- Orange Loaf Cake
- Rhubarb Flapjack Bars
- Upside-down Blackberry and Apple Cake
- Viennese Whirls

INDEX